FAITH AND FAMILY

The Story of Mary Ethel Winfrey

by

Karen Jackson Gabel

Researched by Jeanie Wilson

Published by Karyn Rae Publishing
ISBN: 978-1-946847-92-8

Edited by: Grace Parazzoli
Cover Design by: Humble Nations
Formatting by: Guido Henkel

Printed in the U.S.A.

"A people without the knowledge of their past history, origin and culture is like a tree without roots."

— Marcus Garvey

Table of Contents

About This Book

The memories I have of my childhood days growing up in Siloam Springs, Arkansas, include Sunday-afternoon drives to my grandmother's house. My grandmother, Mary Ethel Winfrey, always lived within driving distance of our home. Those Sunday-afternoon visits usually included aunts and uncles, and I often heard stories about their experiences living on the Colorado prairie. It didn't take too many stories for me to realize that my grandmother's life story needed to be documented in some way, somehow. It wasn't until I completed college, sometime in 1973, that I spent several days with her, writing as fast as I could while she told me her life's story. However, I knew at the time that I would probably not actually write her story until many, many years later, and I told her that. So my notebook, in which I had recorded her story, went into a drawer, where it stayed for forty-three years.

During those years, my husband, Jim, and I raised our two sons, Jimmy and Brandon, while I pursued a career in the medical review profession. It was in 2016, four years after my retirement, that I was casually visiting, via text, with Jeanie Wilson, a friend and former coworker. During that texting exchange, I told Jeanie that I was planning to someday write a book about my grandmother. Jeanie instantly texted back, "You have to do it! Send me names and dates and I will do the research for you." Little did I know that Jeanie is a genealogical research wonder woman—how fortunate for me! So I sent her names and dates, and off we went!

My grandmother told me her story, but without Jeanie's research, I never would have been able to fit all the pieces together. Needless to say, Jeanie Wilson is the reason this book ever got written. Had it not been for her, the story of Mary Ethel Winfrey would still be in a notebook in my desk drawer—**thank you, Jeanie!**

Mary Ethel Winfrey Bailey Whetzel

Her Legacy

This is the story of Mary Ethel Winfrey Bailey Whetzel. **She was the mother of** Robert Leonard Bailey, Jessie O. Bailey Jackson Hayes, Melvel Carl Bailey, Margie Madeline Bailey Ames, and Dortha Mae Bailey Noble Fingerlin. **She was the grandmother of** Douglas Verl Bailey, Frances (Fran) Kay Jackson Henry Endicott, Karen Gayle Jackson Gabel, Garland Todd Jackson, Michael Tabb Jackson, Sondra Lee Bailey Stacks, Melvel Carl Bailey Jr., Donna Jean Bailey Kowalski, Stephen Grey Bailey, Donald Dale Bailey, Barbara Joy Ames Mangrum, Ronda Jo Ames Cunningham, Beverla Sue Noble Hernandez Bailey, Iris Lynn Noble Croft Peevyhouse Mills, and Benny Joan Noble Michael. **She was the great-grandmother of** Eric Alan Bailey, Noel Wade Bailey, Robyn Michelle Bailey Peck, Heather Rey Henry Robison, Barbara (Bobbi) Kay Henry, Bud Douglas Henry II, James (Jimmy) Garland Gabel, Brandon William Gabel, Courtney Leigh Jackson Sloan, Kelsey Marie Jackson Schmidt, Laura Ashley Jackson Long, Jordan Kale Jackson, Kayce Nicole Jackson Pak, Angela Gay Meador, Tammy Kay Pryce, Cynthia Fay Stacks, Jonathan Bailey, Tara Christine Kowalski, Steven Bailey Jr., Jo Ada Bailey, Christopher Lee Bailey, Lana Beth Bailey Riverol, Tina Marie Mangrum, Johnny Daryel Cunningham, James Darren Cunningham, Robert Daniel Hernandez, Angela Yvet Hernandez Coleman, William David Bailey, William Benson Croft, Buffy Jo Croft, Jeromey Jason Croft, Nita Lynn Peevyhouse Gene, Marshall Todd Peevyhouse, Chelsey Nichole Peevyhouse Kreisvelt, Kristian Allen Michael, Kimberly Kathleen Michael, and Erin Rae Michael. **She was the great-great-grandmother of** Hannah Elizabeth

Bailey, Tyler Douglas Peck, Jacob Walker Peck, Bailey Shae Peck, Jonathan David Woods, Jaycee Rey Woods, Eva Frances Henry, Elise Angela Henry, Addison Ann Gabel, Emily James Gabel, Haley Sloane Gabel, Olivia Jackson Gabel, Bailee Cameron Sloan, Hunter Reese Long, Jackson Judd Long, Kale Garland Jackson, Kord Nolan Jackson, Olivia Sun-He Pak, Samson Michael Pak, Aaron Lee Meador, Alyssa Nicole Meador Isam, Barrington Pryce II, LaSondra Nicole Pryce, Aria Renn Schorr, Levi Alan Schorr, Patrick Henry Bailey, Andrew David Bailey, Samantha Nicole Bailey, Ezra Mateo Riverol, Amelia Beth Forrestine Riverol, Noah Bailey, Henry Bailey, Kaitlyn Bailey, Isabella Bailey, Emma Bailey, Bailey Jayden Arnold, Hunter Daryel Dean Cunningham, Hayden Steven Lee Cunningham, Travis Hernandez, Victoria Rain Coleman, Alexandria Coleman, Tara Coleman, Skyler Sage Peevyhouse, Titus Braun, Layden Gene, Jayden Gene, Marlee Peevyhouse, Benson Peevyhouse, Macy Peevyhouse, Keera Stokes, Kayleen Stokes, Kassidy Kreisvelt, Tayla Kreisvelt, Jacob Percy Michael, Grace Michael, and Kate Michael. **She was the great-great-great grandmother of** Cameron Isam, Brady Isam, and Beckham Bailey Isam. **(And the list goes on….)**

Winfrey Lineage Chart
with years of birth and death

Benjamin Henry Winfrey
Born: 1810 Place: Adair County, Kentucky
Marriage to Matilda O. McCain: December 24, 1831
Death: February 1865 Burial: Wakenda Baptist Church Cemetery, Missouri

Children of Benjamin and Matilda McCain Winfrey:
William P. Winfrey (1833–1880)
Florinda M. Winfrey (1834–1929)
Caroline Matilda Winfrey (1837–1909)
Lucinda J. Winfrey (1845–?)
Editha F. Winfrey (1850–1942)
Pina Belle Winfrey (1854–1902)

William P. Winfrey
Born: 1833 Place: Adair County, Kentucky
Parents: Benjamin Winfrey and Matilda O. McCain Winfrey
Marriage to Nancy Elizabeth Cary: November 10, 1853
Death: October 1, 1880 Burial: Wakenda Baptist Church Cemetery, Missouri

Children of William P. and Nancy Cary Winfrey:
James Drake Winfrey (1855–1939)
Creed Benjamin Winfrey (1857–1934)
Ruben S. Winfrey (1858–1900)
Claiborne Jackson Winfrey (1861–1945)
Mary Hester Winfrey (1866–1955)
Alena Belle Winfrey (1870–1950)
Matthew Sherwood Winfrey (1872–1931)

Creed Benjamin Winfrey

Born: 1857 Place: Carroll County, Missouri

Parents: William P. Winfrey and Nancy Elizabeth Cary Winfrey

Marriage to Mary A. Brown: November 13, 1879

Marriage to Blanch May Smith: March 30, 1893

Death: December 3, 1934 Burial: Berryville Memorial Cemetery, Arkansas

Children of Creed Benjamin and Mary Brown Winfrey:

Lillian Mae Winfrey (1880–1955)

Gertrude G. Winfrey (1883–1974)

W. Claude Winfrey (1885–1963)

Harley Glen Winfrey (1889–1966)

Otto Orphus Winfrey (1891–1929)

Children of Creed Benjamin and Blanch Smith Winfrey:

Mary Ethel Winfrey (1894–1987)

Susan Ellen Winfrey (1896–1984)

Nancy Elizabeth Winfrey (1896–1922)

Emil Benjamin Winfrey (1901–1955)

Ruby Estle Winfrey (1910–2004)

Mary Ethel Winfrey

Born: August 30, 1894 Place: Carroll County, Missouri

Parents: Creed Benjamin Winfrey and Blanch Smith Winfrey

Marriage to Leander R. Bailey: January 3, 1914

Death: May 16, 1987 Burial: Allen Cemetery, Oklahoma

Children of Mary Ethel Winfrey Bailey and Leander R. Bailey:

Inez Bailey (November 1, 1914–November 5, 1914) – Born Milan, Missouri

Robert Leonard Bailey (1916–1983) – Born Carrollton, Missouri

Jessie O. Bailey (1919–2009) – Born Andrix, Colorado

Melvel Carl Bailey (1921–2009) – Born Andrix, Colorado

Margie Madeline Bailey (1923–2014) – Born Aguilar, Colorado

Dortha Mae Bailey (1925–2015) – Born St. Joseph, Missouri

FAITH AND FAMILY
The Story of Mary Ethel Winfrey

CHAPTER 1

Eugene Township, near Carrollton, Missouri

LIKE MOST LATE WINTER DAYS IN EUGENE, MISSOURI, THE DAY WAS bright and shiny, but the wind was crisp and cold. The date was March 8, 1906, and Mary Ethel Winfrey had awoken early that morning to the sounds of everyone scurrying around. Even before getting out of bed, Mary Ethel could feel the happiness and excitement in the air, but she instantly knew that she would find it difficult to even pretend to be happy herself. Mae was getting married today, and Mary Ethel did not understand how everyone could be so happy about it. Mae was the first of Creed's children to get married, so of course it was a special occasion. But the idea of Mae leaving was nothing to be happy about, as far as eleven-year-old Mary Ethel was concerned. After all, Mae was the one she depended upon the most.

Getting along without Mae was just not something Mary Ethel could begin to imagine, and it was going to be awfully difficult to hide her sadness because of the closeness of the Winfrey family. Their home on the farm in Eugene Township, Carroll County, had only one bedroom, and in 1906 there were nine Winfrey children, counting Mae. Each night when all the beds were rolled out, the house was wall-to-wall beds. With that kind of closeness, Mary Ethel was going to have to work hard to hide her sorrow.

Mae was marrying Daniel Nugent Lynch, a longtime acquaintance of the Winfrey family. Just like Mae, Dan had grown up in Eugene, and his mother and father, John and Ella Lynch, had always been friends of the Winfrey family. So the marriage of Mae and Dan was a very happy occasion, and Blanch, Mae's stepmother, and Creed, Mae's father, had made plans for a most enjoyable event with all the Winfrey aunts, uncles, cousins, and grandmother Nancy in attendance. And so it was that on March 8, 1906, Mae and Dan got married, a day Mary Ethel would never forget. She liked Dan, and Mae was happy, so somehow she had managed to hide her gloom, at least through the ceremony and the family dinner that followed. But when it came time for Mae and Dan to actually leave for their own home, Mary Ethel could no longer keep her emotions in check. Rather than let Mae see her sadness, she headed for the apple tree she had climbed so many times before—the apple tree Mae used to always find her in. From her favorite perch in that old tree, she could see them depart, and because the budding leaves gave her a little bit of solitude, she could finally cry.

Mae, whose full name was Lillian Mae Winfrey, was Mary Ethel's half-sister and the oldest of Creed's ten children. She was born in 1880, and the first eleven years of her life had been what most people of the time would have called a perfect childhood. Her mother, Mary Alice Brown, had married her father, Creed Benjamin Winfrey, in 1879, and Mae was born the following year. Three years later, Gertrude Grace, whom everyone called Gertie, was born. William Claude, named for his grandfather and called Claude, was born two years after Gertie, and Harley Glendon was born four years after Claude.

When Harley was born, Mae was nine years old, and life on the family farm was good. Eugene was just a small farm community, but it was near Carrollton, the county seat of Carroll County, Missouri, and Carrollton was a thriving small city with a population of 2,313 the year Mae was born. By the time Mae was ten years old, the population of Carrollton had increased to almost 4,000, a telephone exchange and a waterworks plant had been built, and coal oil lamps were slowly being replaced with electric lightbulbs. Because Carrollton was located on the line of the Wabash, St. Louis & Pacific railroad, commerce was steadily on the rise.

The city of Carrollton had been designed with the county courthouse in the middle of a square, surrounded by businesses. Banks, produce markets, dry goods stores, a drugstore, a hotel, a hardware store, and a millinery store could all be found in Carrollton in 1890, and two factories, the Chapman & Dewey Box Factory and the Coffey & Staley Furniture Factory, were being established. Multiple area newspapers kept the people of Carroll County informed about all the local and national news, and Carrollton could boast a church for almost every religious persuasion. Of significant importance to Mae, Carrollton had two schools, one of which she was attending. Mae, at the age of ten, had already decided that someday, she would be a teacher.

Carroll County was one of those places that people often referred to as "God's country." It is described in *History of Carroll County, Missouri*, published by Hearthstone Legacy Publications thus: "To native Missourians…Missouri is the garden of the world and Carroll County is the garden of Missouri." The county is bordered on the south by the Missouri River, and its eastern boundary is the Grand River. *History of Carroll County, Missouri* goes on to describe this "garden" as follows: "The depth and richness of the soil on the Missouri river bottoms is a wonder…and it seems that extended droughts like the one that spread over a great portion of the United States, during the summer of 1881, had no effect in cutting short the crops of this wonderfully fertile region." Another important water source for this fertile region is the Wakanda River, which runs through Carroll County and into the Missouri River. This river is depicted in *History of Carroll County, Missouri* in impressive detail:

> From the bluffs that skirt the meanderings of the Waconda, a panorama of beauty unfolds to the eye…. Leaving the base of this whole line of bluffs extending southeasterly, the turbid waters of the Wy-a-con-da (Wakanda), flow sluggishly and pour into the Missouri. Campbell's Gazeteer of Missouri, revised edition, says: "The Wakanda abounded with fine fish, and on its banks and in the adjacent timber were found deer, elk, buffalo, turkeys and other game in abundance. The Indians, thinking that a stream where the Great Spirit had placed such quantities of game and fish, must be sacred, dared not destroy or kill anything in the

> neighborhood, except on festival days, and their festivities were always held on the banks of this river, bearing its name 'Wakanda,' meaning God's river.

The richness of Carroll County is further described:

> There is scarcely a variety of surface, valley timber, bluff or prairie, but can be found in this county, and taking the position, climate, and general facilities, it can be made one of the finest stock raising counties in the west, besides the climatic influences and adaptability of the soil for all kinds of grains, vegetables, fruits, and grasses, are unsurpassed, and the statistics of late years establish the fact that Carroll, in proportion to its general area and population, is second to no county in the United States in the production of corn, oats, wheat, hemp, tobacco, fruits, cattle, horses, and hogs.

As far as the Creed Benjamin Winfrey family was concerned, Carroll County lived up to its promises. By 1890, Creed had cultivated a successful farm that produced food for his family, grain for his stock, and tobacco as a cash crop. Together he and Mary were fully engaged in the raising of four active children. The work was not easy, and they were not rich, but they were a comfortable and happy family.

By 1890, Mae had found that she loved going to school and was staying completely occupied with her studies and the work that was required of a ten-year-old girl on the farm. It was probably sometime in September 1890, soon after Mae had started the third grade and Gertie had started first, that another happy family announcement was made: Mary was expecting their fifth child. Boys were important to farming families; in all likelihood, Creed was hoping for a third son. In February 1891, another baby boy, Otto Orphus Winfrey, came into the Winfrey family. Yet the joyous occasion immediately turned to days full of fear. Otto's birth had been tremendously difficult, and Mary was having a hard time. Family members came and went, always leaving with a look of fear and sorrow on their faces, and after a few days, Mae began to understand what those looks meant. After spending five weeks in bed following Otto's birth, Mary died. She was thirty years old.

In just five weeks everything changed for Creed and his family. He was now, at the age of thirty-four, the father of five motherless children, all under the age of twelve. And with no warning or preparation, Mae became responsible for her four younger siblings: Gertie, who was eight, Claude (six), Harley (almost two), and Otto, the newborn. Mae's childhood, at the age of eleven, was suddenly and completely over.

***

CREED BENJAMIN WINFREY WAS WELL KNOWN AND WELL RESPECTED in Carroll County. His family had been there since long before the Civil War. His grandfather and grandmother, Benjamin Henry Winfrey and Matilda O. McCain Winfrey, were married in 1831 in Adair County, Kentucky; their firstborn, William P. Winfrey, was Creed's father. William and his younger sister Florinda were both born in Kentucky. When William was four years old and Florinda was almost two, probably sometime in mid-1836, the family of four—Benjamin, Matilda, William, and Florinda—made their way on horseback from Adair County, Kentucky, to Carroll County, Missouri, most likely crossing the Mississippi River at St. Louis. They left Kentucky with the expectation of staking a land claim in Missouri. After settling on a spot in the Grand River Township area of Carroll County, they began to build a log cabin. Soon, possibly even before the cabin was completed, their third child, Caroline, was born. Once Benjamin and Matilda—today considered true pioneers of Carroll County—were settled in their new home, they filed their land claim of eighty acres in District 15 of Carroll County, on January 10, 1840. And of course, their family continued to grow. By 1856, Lucinda, Editha, and Pina had been born, completing their family of six children—one son and five daughters.

After arriving in Missouri in 1836, Benjamin and Matilda spent the next twenty years farming the fertile fields of Carroll County and raising their family. Their first eighteen years there were productive and peaceful, with the exception of a short period in 1838. Having not been made welcome in Independence, Missouri, the Mormon followers of Joseph Smith fled into Carroll, Clay, and Caldwell Counties in Missouri, buying property but not revealing that they were Mormons. The Mormons purchased property in and around DeWitt, near Benjamin and Matilda's farm, and Mormon settlers soon began to move into the DeWitt area in great numbers. When the people of Carroll County became aware that the Mormons were there, they expressed great eagerness for the immediate removal of the Mormons from the county. Two public meetings were held in Carrollton in July 1838, resulting in the determination that the people of Carroll County would, with the help of neighbors from the surrounding counties, make it completely clear to the Mormons that they must leave DeWitt. If they refused to leave peacefully, forcible expulsion would be the next step. Soon a meeting was arranged with elected Carroll County officials and Mormon leaders, yet attempted negotiations during that meeting led to no agreement. The Mormon leaders let it be known that they had no intention of ever leaving DeWitt, under any circumstances.

The men of Carroll and many surrounding counties, therefore, began to form county militias. On September 21, 1838, these militias gathered around DeWitt and engaged in one of the battles of what became known as the Missouri Mormon War. The conflict at DeWitt included some exchanges of gunfire and lasted several days. When a cannon arrived from Jackson County, and the number of militiamen grew to well over five hundred, the Mormon settlers accepted the terms offered to them, loaded up their wagons, and left DeWitt.

Other Mormon conflicts erupted in nearby Missouri counties. Eventually the governor of Missouri, Lilburn W. Boggs, called out the state militia, instructing them to resolve the Mormon issue and, if necessary, expel them from the state. In October 1838, Joseph Smith and other Mormon leaders surrendered, and the rest of the Mormons were told to leave the state with their families. Having been invited to Illinois, they settled the town of Nauvoo, Illinois, on the Mississippi River. By 1844, the year Joseph Smith was killed, the population of Nauvoo had risen to twelve thousand Mormons, rivaling the size of

Chicago. But in Missouri, by May 1839, not a family of Mormons remained, and the peaceful lives of the people of Carroll County resumed—for a while.

It was sometime during the year 1854 when the question of slavery began affecting the people of Carroll County, and the winds of civil war began to blow. Missouri had entered the Union in 1821 as a slave state, under the provisions of the Missouri Compromise. The Missouri Compromise allowed Missouri to join the Union as a slave state only because Maine was entering as a free state—the goal being that the number of free states would stay equal to the number of slave states. However, the Kansas-Nebraska Act, passed in 1854, allowed people in the territories of Kansas and Nebraska to decide for themselves whether to allow slavery within their borders. By 1855, the question of whether Kansas would enter the Union as a slave state or a free state came to dominate public life. Missourians were so deeply involved in the issue that many families migrated to Kansas to try to influence its future.

During 1855 and 1856, tensions erupted into open warfare between proslavery and antislavery forces in Kansas. In May 1856, the violence escalated when a group of Missouri settlers who had moved into Kansas were killed during a massacre at Pottawatomie Creek. The massacre was led by John Brown and his group of abolitionists. The warfare that erupted in Kansas accounted for much of the tension that led up to the Civil War. Those episodes of violence were reported in great detail in the *Carrollton Democrat*, the only newspaper in Carroll County at the time. Then in 1858, newspapers across the country began reporting on the debates between Stephen Douglas and Abraham Lincoln, who were running for a US Senate seat. Douglas won, but the debates elevated Lincoln—and his antislavery views—to national prominence, and on November 6, 1860, Lincoln was elected president of the United States.

In response to Lincoln's election, the state of South Carolina declared, on December 20, 1860, that it was leaving the Union. Lincoln was inaugurated on March 4, 1861, and on April 12 of that year, Fort Sumter, in the harbor at Charleston, South Carolina, was attacked by

Confederate guns. The American Civil War had begun. On June 8, 1861, ten additional Southern states announced their secession from the Union. The eleven seceding states together formed the Confederate States of America.

Even though Missouri was a slave state, it did not secede from the Union. The stance in Missouri was that of complete neutrality—to join neither the North nor the South. When President Lincoln called on the Union states to contribute to a 75,000-man militia, and specifically asked the state of Missouri for four regiments, the governor of Missouri, Claiborne F. Jackson, sent a letter of refusal to Secretary of War Simon Cameron stating:

> There can be, I apprehend, no doubt but these men are intended to form a part of the President's army to make war upon the people of the seceded states. Your requisition, in my judgement, is illegal, unconstitutional and revolutionary; in it objects, inhuman and diabolical, and cannot be complied with. Not one man will Missouri furnish to carry on such an unholy crusade.

Instead of sending men to fight with the Union Army, the individual counties of Missouri once again began assembling county militias—this time in an attempt to keep both Union and Confederate soldiers out of the state.

The Civil War took a toll on Carroll County, despite efforts to remain neutral, but in comparison to other areas, the people of the county were fortunate to live where they did during those days. After Carrollton was established as the county seat, probably around 1834, the town began to steadily grow. However, *History of Carroll County, Missouri* records:

> The war coming on…not only impeded the progress of the place, but through the bitterness engendered by the sentiments for and against the established government, many of the citizens left, and the town in a measure became deserted. Excitement ran higher as the war came on and the town gradually lost its vigor. Demoralization and dilapidation

> followed. Legal authority was defied, and a spirit of lawlessness took the place of obedience.... Roving bands of lawless men, sometimes Federal, sometimes Confederate, would visit the town weekly, sometimes oftener, and ride through the streets firing revolvers and threatening the lives of the citizens, causing every business man to lock up his premises for hours. This state of affairs lasted so long that the charter of the town was forfeited, and there was scarcely the shadow of a town government known or respected.

When the war began, Benjamin Winfrey, having been born in Kentucky in 1810, was about fifty-one years old, yet he eventually completed the necessary papers to register with the Union Army. However, by that time he was quite incapacitated with rheumatoid arthritis. Even though he was never a soldier, he nevertheless became a victim of the war. Benjamin died in February 1865, less than three months before Robert E. Lee's surrender at the Appomattox Court House on April 9, 1865, which marked the end of the Civil War. *History of Carroll County, Missouri* records the death of Benjamin Winfrey as follows:

> What apology is to be offered for the killing of poor old Benjamin Winfrey by the Militia, in February, 1865. It appears that in that month two Militia men called at Winfrey's house in the night and represented that they had orders to take him to DeWitt. Winfrey was sick in bed at the time, but got up and clothed himself, believing that he had been sent for by Captain Morris Schnapp at DeWitt. When they got about three hundred yards east of the house, without a word of warning they shot him four times before he fell. After he fell they fired five more shots at his head as they supposed, but when the wounded man was found by his friends, it proved that the shots that were fired after he fell went through Winfrey's cap that had fallen and dropped close to his head, it being night they mistook the cap for his head. Winfrey lived four days after being wounded. He was an inoffensive old gentleman about fifty years of age and badly crippled with

> the rheumatism. Captain Schnapp hearing of the affair investigated the case and found it was not his men who had murdered Winfrey. Had it been, Schnapp would have arrested them and had them tried by drum-head court martial.

The militiamen who murdered Benjamin were of the so-called Anderson's Raiders, a group of Confederates who engaged in guerilla warfare throughout the Civil War. Benjamin was buried near his farm in the cemetery of the Wakenda Baptist Church, which he and Matilda had helped establish. He was killed just a few weeks before Abraham Lincoln was assassinated at Ford's Theater on April 14, 1865.

William P. Winfrey, Benjamin's son and Creed's father, had married Nancy Elizabeth Cary on December 31, 1853, about seven years before the start of the war. When the Civil War began, he and Nancy had three sons: James Drake, who was six, Creed Benjamin, who was four, and Ruben, who was three. Nancy was pregnant with their fourth child, who was named Claiborne Jackson Winfrey upon his birth, in honor of the then-governor of Missouri. After Benjamin's murder, William and Nancy stayed on the Grand River farm, raising their family and caring for William's mother, Matilda. Three of William's sisters—Florinda, Lucinda, and Editha—had married and were living in and around Carroll County. His other two sisters, Caroline and Pina, did not marry but instead stayed with their mother and brother, helping on the family farm. Matilda lived to be seventy-nine years old, dying in 1892. She was also buried at the Wakenda Baptist Church Cemetery.

When the Civil War, and all the heartbreak that went with it, finally ended, Carrollton and Carroll County began to recover quickly. After the war, William and Nancy had three more children: Mary Hester, Alena Belle, and Matthew Sherwood. It is unknown what caused William's illness, but on the 1880 census he was described as being "almost wholly paralyzed," and on October 1, 1880, at the age of forty-seven, he died. His youngest child, Matthew, was only seven years old. He did live to see his first grandchild, Mae. Mae was less than two months old when he died.

Creed was the first of William and Nancy's children to wed. He married his childhood sweetheart Mary (née Mary Alice Brown), the year before his father died. Creed farmed the land, and he and Mary started raising their family in the same area of Carroll County as his father. And life was good—until the tragedy of Mary's death on March 15, 1891, which changed everything. News of her death traveled quickly, and everyone in the surrounding area was well aware of Creed's sudden unfortunate circumstances. But thankfully, there was family nearby—lots and lots of family. Creed's four brothers, James, Reuben, Claiborne, and Matthew, and his two sisters, Hester and Alena, were all living in or near Carrollton. Yet despite plenty of help from Creed's brothers and sisters, Mae, at the age of eleven, had to instantly transform into a mother figure for her four young siblings, including six-week-old Otto.

The unexpected death of her mother left Mae feeling grief stricken, frightened, and helpless. For days, she didn't think it could possibly be true, but then, when the relatives quit coming so often, she knew she had to acknowledge the difficult truth. Her life was now completely different, and her father needed her. With disappointment, she accepted the fact that she would not be going to school for a while. But knowing that her sister and three brothers depended on her so much made school no longer seem so important—it would have to wait. What was important was that they make it through this terrible time together. So she set her mind to the tasks at hand, those of the day-in and day-out care requirements of four young children who had just lost their mother. She cooked what she knew how to cook and learned to cook more. She washed and mended clothes, and she learned by trial and error how to care for a newborn baby. She made sure that Gertie continued with school, and in the fall of the next year, when Claude started first grade and Gertie started third, Mae was able to return to school to begin her fourth-grade year. It was a difficult time, but they made it through. And then, two years and fifteen days after Mary died, everything changed—again.

CHAPTER 2

1893 to 1902: A New Beginning

WITH ALL OF CREED'S BROTHERS AND SISTERS LIVING SO NEARBY, THE search for a new wife for Creed, and a mother for his children, must have begun immediately. Little is known about where Blanch came from or how Creed met her, but on March 30, 1893, just over two years after Mary's death, Creed Benjamin, at age thirty-seven, married fifteen-year-old Blanch May Smith, the daughter of Ralph Skidmore Smith and Susan Mary Miller Smith. They were married by a justice of the peace in Cooper County, Missouri, with Blanch's father, Ralph, in attendance. Ralph gave his consent to the marriage, which was required because Blanch was under the age of eighteen. Blanch turned sixteen on April 7, one week after the wedding.

So once again Creed's brothers and sisters gathered, but this time it was to wish Creed and Blanch a happy life together, and to express their joy that little Otto, now two years old, had someone to call Mother. Even though nothing is known about how Blanch came into the lives of the Creed B. Winfrey family, it can be assumed that she must have needed the Winfrey family, maybe even as much as the Winfrey family needed her. Perhaps difficult circumstances had caused Blanch to need Creed, but whatever her situation had been, she was probably not prepared for the challenges that lay ahead. At barely sixteen, she had become the wife of a thirty-seven-year-old man and the stepmother to five children—three of whom remembered their mother very well, and one who was just three years younger than herself. Finding herself in the situation of having to fill such a tremendous void in the lives of six people must have been all but overwhelming. Despite the fact that she was so desperately needed, and despite the relief that her presence surely brought to the family, there were undoubtedly emotions to deal with and obstacles to work through for all seven of them, and probably especially for Blanch. But all accounts of Blanch indicate that she was an extremely remarkable person, and it undoubtedly did not take long for her to realize what an extraordinary family she was now a member of. Slowly, things began to take on a new sense of normalcy for everyone in the family—somehow, together, they began to make it work.

The most important aspect of returning to normal was the family's evening meals. After Mary's death, suppertime was the most difficult time of each day for everyone. Mae did her best to do what needed to be done, but when the family sat down for supper each evening, Mary's absence was all that any of them could think about. There was just too much sadness. So when Blanch joined the family, her youthful interest in what everyone was doing brought a joy to the supper table that had been terribly missed for a long time. Gradually, everyone began to want to tell her about their day, and after a while, the evening meals once again became a happy time of family togetherness, the most important part of the day. And fortunately for Creed and his family, thanks to his farm, there was *always* food on the supper table.

Even though 1893 was the year of a new beginning for the Creed B. Winfrey family, it was a year of national crisis in the United States. In February, a month before Creed and Blanch were married, what became known as the Panic of 1893 was set off by the collapse of two of the country's largest employers: the Philadelphia and Reading Railroad and the National Cordage Company. Following the failure of these companies, a panic erupted on the stock market, and soon banks and investment firms began calling in loans, causing hundreds of business bankruptcies across the country, including railroads, banks, and steel mills. People began rushing to withdraw their money from banks. In March 1893, Grover Cleveland was inaugurated as president of the United States for a second time. (He had been president from 1885 to 1889 and was the only president to serve nonconsecutive terms.)

Cleveland spent his entire second term attempting to deal with this serious economic depression. During that time, five hundred banks closed, over fifteen thousand businesses failed, and large farms ceased operations.

Despite the national crisis, Creed, Blanch, and the children were able to remain focused on getting their lives back to normal. Two months after Creed and Blanch were married, Mae finished her fourth-grade year in school, Gertie finished her third-grade year, and Claude completed the first grade. They attended the Rosebud School, which was located in the area known as the Winfrey Grove. It was three miles from the Winfrey home, and Mae, Gertie, and Claude walked the distance together. Blanch was eager for all the children to go to school because she had never been able to attend herself, and as soon as Mae became aware of this fact, her teaching instincts set in. Each evening, after the dishes were washed and put away, Mae and Blanch would keep one coal oil lamp burning as they worked on Mae's homework assignments together. These late evenings of study became a bond between them, so it is not surprising that sometime in February 1894, Mae was the first to learn that the family of seven would soon be a family of eight. Not long after Blanch told Mae that she was expecting, Blanch and Creed made the happy announcement to the entire family—around the supper table.

Since Creed and his brothers and sisters were such a close-knit family, it was probably a disappointment for Blanch when she was unable to attend the first big family event to take place after her marriage to Creed. On August 23, 1894, Creed's youngest brother, Matthew, got married. Seven days later, Blanch gave birth to her first and Creed's sixth child, Mary Ethel.

With the birth of Mary Ethel, the one-bedroom house on the Winfrey farm once again got a little bit smaller. By that time, the dining room had been Mae and Gertie's bedroom for quite a while. Each night, they would push back the table and chairs, pull curtains over the doors, and roll out their feather beds. The three boys slept on the screened back porch whenever weather permitted, but in the winter, their beds were rolled out onto the kitchen floor—as close to the stove as they could safely get. Once Mary Ethel could sleep unattended, it became necessary for the living room to serve double duty as a living room by day and a bedroom by night.

However, she did not sleep in the living room by herself for long. When Mary Ethel was two years old, on May 23, 1896, Blanch gave birth to identical twin girls. They were named Nancy Elizabeth, after Creed's mother Nancy, and Susan Ellen, after Blanch's mother Susan. Soon beds were being rolled out for Mary Ethel, Nancy, and Susan (Sue) in any available spot in the living room. By mid-1896, the Creed B. Winfrey family was a family of ten.

Mary Ethel's life growing up on the Eugene farm was just like that of most farm kids. She and her brothers and sisters were all expected to help with the chores. The boys helped with the farming and livestock, while the girls cooked, canned, and learned to sew at an early age. They were also expected to do well in school, which was not an option for any of the Winfrey children—they were all required to attend. In the spring of 1897, Mae graduated from the eighth grade, the highest grade level available in the public schools in Carroll County at the time.

Sunday school was also not an option for the Winfrey children. Creed and Blanch faithfully attended church every Sunday with their family, just as the Winfreys before them had done. Wakenda Baptist Church was their place of worship and an essential part of their spiritual and social lives. The Bible was not only taught in church; it was also taught in school. The Winfrey children were raised to rely on the Bible for answers to their questions, fears, and concerns.

In the spring of 1897, just before Mae graduated, William McKinley was inaugurated as the twenty-fifth president of the United States. Running on a platform of promoting American prosperity, McKinley triumphed easily over Democrat William Jennings Bryan. Americans saw McKinley as the answer to the crippling economic depression brought on by the Panic of 1893.

Not long after McKinley took office, the national news began to focus on Cuba, a longtime colony of Spain. Following the American Civil War, American businessmen began monopolizing the sugar and tobacco markets in Cuba; by 1894, 90 percent of Cuba's total exports went to the United States, and the United States provided 40 percent of all Cuba's imports. Spain held political authority over Cuba, but economic authority there was shifting to the United States. In 1895, a revolt for Cuban independence from Spain began to harm important US economic interests, and after McKinley's election, powerful businessmen began to press him to seek an end to the uprising. Because of this pressure, McKinley sent the USS *Maine* to Havana to help ensure the safety of American citizens and American interests. On February 15, 1898, the *Maine*, after suffering a massive explosion, sank in Havana Harbor, killing 267 of the 355 American sailors onboard. American newspapers blamed the explosion on Spain, and on April 21, 1898, the US Navy began a blockade of Cuba. In response to the blockade, Spain declared war on the United States; on April 25, Congress declared war on Spain.

The Spanish-American War was short lived, lasting less than four months, and was an easy victory for the United States. The American victory resulted in the signing of the Treaty of Paris on December 10, 1898, in which Spain renounced all claim to Cuba, ceded Guam and Puerto Rico to the United States, and transferred sovereignty over the Philippines to the United States. America emerged from the war as a world power, with multiple overseas possessions and a new stake in international politics. The war also provided the stage upon which Theodore Roosevelt and his Rough Riders rose to national prominence.

Gertie completed the eighth grade in the spring of 1898. In the fall of that year, all three Winfrey boys were attending the Rosebud School. Claude was in the seventh grade, Harley was in the third, and Otto had started the first grade. It was in January 1899, when Mary Ethel was four and a half years old, that the schools around Carrollton were closed, and the people of the area were told to stay in their homes. Much to everyone's astonishment, several people in the nearby town of Bosworth had been diagnosed with smallpox, and it was spreading to Carrollton. The smallpox vaccine had been made a requirement in all states by the 1850s; however, it was a requirement that was difficult to enforce. People, including many physicians, feared that the vaccine was more dangerous than the disease itself, and therefore many were not vaccinated. By 1897, the dreaded disease had largely been eliminated from the United States, but not entirely. At the beginning of the outbreak in Bosworth, the local physician had failed to recognize the disease, and it spread rapidly. By January 1899, Bosworth was under a complete quarantine.

Fortunately, when the disease was found to have spread to Carrollton, Carrollton was ready. The County Board of Health quickly closed the schools, and all general movement of the population was stopped. Businesses were paralyzed; people stayed confined to their homes for three months. Anxiety and fear gripped the entire county. The outbreak resulted in twelve deaths: ten in Bosworth and two in Carrollton. By the end of March, the newspapers reported that the spread of the disease had been stopped, and the quarantines were lifted. The Winfrey family received this news with great relief. Everyone was healthy, and they could finally leave the farm. Several members of the family had not been vaccinated, so that was corrected as soon as news arrived that the vaccine was available.

The two years after the smallpox outbreak, 1900 and 1901, were eventful. The area newspapers were full of exciting reports of telephones, electric lighting, and automobiles. It was soon after Mary Ethel's sixth birthday, sometime in September 1900, that Blanch and Creed announced that the family was growing again. Blanch was expecting child number nine, and on April 13, 1901, much to Creed's joy, the Winfrey family welcomed another boy, Emil Benjamin Winfrey. The Creed B. Winfrey family was now a family of eleven.

Just before the fall school term of 1901, Mae's dream of becoming a school teacher came true. She was hired to teach at a school near Carrollton. She was finally, officially a teacher! That September, Mae started her teaching career, and Mary Ethel joined her brothers Harley and Otto on the three-mile trek to the Rosebud School. The start of her first-grade year was quite memorable because it occurred at a historic time in US history. School had barely gotten underway when the news came, on September 6, that the president of the United States, William McKinley, had been shot at the Pan-American Exposition in

Buffalo, New York. Six days later, he died of complications from his bullet wounds, and Vice President Theodore Roosevelt became president. For a while, that was just about the only thing that was talked about at school and at home—around the supper table.

CHAPTER 3

1903 to 1909: The Floods

IN JUNE 1903, THE WINFREY FARM CAME INTO EXTREME JEOPARDY FOR the first time. At the beginning of the spring planting season, it appeared that the growing season was going to be a great one. Spring was particularly wet, and everyone was predicting bumper crops. By the end of May, all the crops had been planted; that hard work was behind them. But in late June, it started to rain again—better said, it began to pour—and pour it did for days. *Twentieth Century History of Carroll County, Missouri*, by S. K. Turner and S. A. Clark, provides a detailed description of the situation:

> June, 1903, witnessed the highest rise in creeks and rivers ever known in Carroll county and damage beyond computation was inflicted upon stock and growing crops. To the unprecedented waters of the Missouri river were added the swollen creeks and smaller rivers along its entire length and when the river was full to overflowing there was no place for the water of the tributaries, which spread out over the low lands so that it was one vast expanse of water from bluff to bluff, broken only by the railroad embankment in places and the extreme high points of bottom lands. The houses were nearly all depopulated, the inhabitants having been taken to the uplands where the houses and barns were thrown open to the refugees who were taken care of. Many lost all they had and aid committees were organized to extend help to the unfortunate ones. It was estimated that sixty-five thousand

> acres were flooded, of which fifteen thousand acres was in wheat and twenty thousand acres had been prepared for corn or had been planted. The loss was estimated at three hundred and twenty-five thousand dollars for Carroll county, on crops alone.

Three hundred and twenty-five thousand dollars in 1903 would be equal to well over eight million dollars in 2018.

Once again, Creed's brothers and sisters banded together to help each other out—the flood had affected them all. They joined forces and began the difficult task of bringing their farms back to life. And their efforts paid off. By the next year's planting season, things were back to normal, and the harvest of 1904 produced the usual bounty. Life for the Winfrey families was back on track.

Following the flood, Mary Ethel began to notice that the talks around the supper table were changing. The flood had started entirely new conversations about free land on the Great Plains of Colorado, and about the good money that could be made in the Oklahoma wheat fields. Mary Ethel noticed that Claude, now eighteen, was the one who was most eager to talk about these things.

The opportunity to acquire free land in the United States had been a possibility since the first Homestead Act was passed in 1862. That act gave an applicant the opportunity to own 160 acres of land, called a homestead, at little or no cost. Millions of acres of public land, primarily in the midwestern part of the United States, were made available to homestead, and soon after the Homestead Act of 1862 was passed, many people began traveling to the Midwest to stake their claims. But talks at the Winfrey house about staking claims on the Great Plains were just that—merely talk.

In May 1904, Harley completed his eighth-grade year of school, and that summer, Gertie was hired to teach at the Rosebud School for the school term of 1904–1905. That September Gertie began her teaching career, and four of her students were her own siblings: Otto was in the seventh grade, Mary Ethel in fourth, and Nancy and Sue in second, all at the Rosebud School.

In the spring of 1905, it appeared that the upcoming farming season was going to be a good one. Recovery efforts brought on by the flood of 1903 were complete, and that flood was well in the past. Mary Ethel, now nine years old, was liking school very much. Sometime during her fifth-grade year, Archie Bachtel became an especially important friend to her. Archie, who was at the same grade level as Mary Ethel, was the reason she liked school so much. Also that spring, Mae's courtship with Dan Lynch was growing more serious. Dan's father, John A. Lynch, was a highly successful farmer, operating a 480-acre farm in the bottomlands near Carrollton, very near the Winfrey farm. A serious relationship between Mae and Dan was no surprise to anyone.

However, in September 1905, near the end of the harvest season, the bottomland of Carroll County flooded again. This flood is described in *Twentieth Century History of Carroll County, Missouri*:

> Thursday, September 24, 1905, and a few days following, saw the waters of Wakenda creek higher in places than had been known before since 1844. Fortunately, the river was not so high and the water had a good chance to get away. The downpour of rain was general all over the county, but seemed to be more severe in the western portion of the county on the headwaters of the Wakenda and Turkey creek. Bridges were washed out all over the county and great damage done to growing crops and farm interests in general.

This flood was particularly hard on the wheat and corn crops; Dan reported that more than half of his family's wheat crop and a large portion of their growing corn crop had been lost. And at the Winfrey super table, the conversation once again turned to the free land on the Great Plains of Colorado, and the money that could be made in the Oklahoma wheat harvest.

Then, much to Mae and the Winfrey family's surprise, Dan's father, John, decided to leave Missouri in the hopes of finding better farmland in a drier area. After discovering that the farming opportunities in Ponca City, Oklahoma, were not up to their expectations, John and Ella moved to a farm in Anderson County, Kansas. In the fall of 1905, Dan left Eugene to join his family in Kansas.

The flood of 1905 made things difficult for Creed and his family, but it was not as bad as what they had experienced in 1903. At least the early part of the 1905 growing season had produced some good crops, so they had food for the coming winter. The family worked together again to clean up the flood damage, and life went on.

Mary Ethel started her sixth-grade year of school that fall, and one of the most memorable events of her life happened in October of that year. One Saturday in mid-October, the nearby town of Bosworth held a farmer's carnival. Hundreds of people from Carroll County and other surrounding counties attended—including the entire Winfrey family. It was like nothing Mary Ethel had ever experienced. There was a grand parade with beautiful floats, and a band played music throughout the entire carnival. There were sideshows and amusement rides that provided entertainment many had never seen before. But best of all, Archie Bachtel was there, and he spent the day with Mary Ethel and her family. It was at the end of that day that she knew for sure: she was his girlfriend. That made her happy.

That fall, Mae continued on with her school-teaching career, but she taught during most of the school year of 1905 with a heavy heart. Dan's leaving had been a complete surprise, and she missed him terribly. Gertie also continued to teach school that fall. She taught at the Rosebud School for only one year. In the fall of 1905, she taught at the Winfrey School, a rural school built on land that had been donated by her great-grandfather, Benjamin. Because of the distance of the school from home, Gertie had to board near the school, but she always came home on the weekends.

Mae did not have to endure her sadness over Dan's departure for long. Early in 1906, Dan returned to the Lynch farm. His family was still in Kansas, but his heart was in Eugene, and soon after he returned, he asked Mae to marry him. Not long after Mae and Dan became engaged, Dan's family also returned to Carroll County. It hadn't taken Dan's father long to decide that Kansas was the poorest farming country on earth. He too made the decision to return to Carroll County, where at least a living could be made—in spite of the floods.

The year 1906 was almost as eventful as 1905, especially with Mae and Dan's wedding in March of that year. That fall Mary Ethel started her seventh-grade school year, and Emil started the first grade, so it was Mary Ethel, Nancy, Sue, and Emil who were now making the three-mile walk to school. This was a special time for Mary Ethel—she loved going to school, where she got to see Archie every day.

Gertie taught two years at the Winfrey School, but for the school term of 1907–1908, she accepted a position at the Cary School. The Cary School was a rural school built on land donated by the family of Creed's mother, Nancy Cary Winfrey.

In the spring of 1908, just before Mary Ethel finished her eighth-grade year, Harley decided that he was going to Oklahoma to work the wheat harvest. He left right away, assuring his family that he would return just as soon as the harvest was over. Then, in June, about two months after Harley left for Oklahoma, the farmlands of Carroll County were once again destroyed by flood waters. *Twentieth Century History of Carroll County, Missouri* describes the flood of 1908:

> June 11, 1908, the Missouri river again overflowed many acres of land adjacent to its banks, the water being higher than at any time since the flood of 1903. The levees which had been constructed were strengthened in hopes that they would withstand the force of the waters, but they were insufficient to stand, and devastation and ruin swept fine crops from thousands of acres of land. The waters continued to rise for almost a week with continued rains and new floods from the upper river regions constantly coming down.

Once again, the primary subject of conversations around the Winfrey supper table turned to long discussions about free land on the Great Plains of Colorado. Now it wasn't just Claude who was extremely interested in these prospects. Creed and Otto were also joining in the conversations, with what appeared to Mary Ethel to be much enthusiasm.

Gertie had some news of her own for the family that summer. She had been offered, and had accepted, a teaching position at the Hazel Dell School, near Braymer, Missouri. Braymer was about forty miles from the Winfrey farm, and she would be moving there before the start of the school term.

For quite some time prior to the 1908 flood, newspapers and magazines had been reporting on the success of what was called the dryland farming movement. Lands that had previously been thought useful only for grazing were now reported to be valuable for agriculture, as farmers were adopting techniques of deep plowing, compacting, summer fallowing (deep plowing land in the summer but not sowing it until the following spring), and planting drought-resistant crops—primarily wheat, corn, and beans. All of these reports were eagerly studied by Creed and his sons, and were always discussed in detail at the supper table.

The flood of 1908 had left the Winfrey family with the prospect of a lean winter ahead. By late fall, Harley had returned from what was considered a successful summer in the Oklahoma wheat fields, and reports of productive dryland farming on free land in Colorado were making that state very inviting. But still, Creed and his family stayed. They cleaned up after this third flood in an attempt to get things back to normal, and they prepared as best they could for the winter ahead.

During that lean winter, on February 19, 1909, news came that the Enlarged Homestead Act had been passed. This act increased the maximum permissible number of acres of land for homesteading from 160 to 320, in parts of Colorado and several other states. When this news arrived, the conversations around the Winfrey supper table were full of excitement, and plans began to be made.

By the planting season of 1909, things were back to normal once again, but normal did not last long. That next July the rains came again, and once again the farmers of Carroll County suffered great losses. *Twentieth Century History of Carroll County, Missouri* describes the flood of 1909 with extreme detail:

> Wednesday, July 14, 1909, the waters of Grand river reached a point never before touched. A wall of water came down the river carrying destruction to grain, stock and property before it. The railroads were washed out and untold damage was done. The Missouri river was at a very high stage, yet the levees nearly all withstood the strain and held. Grand river overflowed the whole of Smith township and caused the current of the Missouri to actually flow up stream for several miles. The lateness of the season made it impossible to put out new crops, which added to the burdens of the stricken districts. Relief committees were organized and Carroll county took care of her own unfortunates.

This was the fourth major flood in the past seven years, and the Creed B. Winfrey family had had enough. Claude was now twenty-four years old and Harley was twenty, and the decision to go to Colorado to stake land claims for 320 acres was an easy one for both of them. By August, they had their wagons packed with everything they believed they needed to successfully dryland farm. That month, they left for Colorado. The day Claude and Harley left was a day of mixed emotions for the entire family. There was excitement over the prospect of them going to Colorado to a better life, but sadness pervaded as well. Everyone knew there was no expectation that they would return.

In September, following Claude and Harley's departure, Nancy and Sue started the eighth grade, and Emil started the fourth. The national news that was getting everyone's attention, near the end of 1909, was that Henry Ford was mass-producing Model T Fords, and they were becoming somewhat affordable.

The year closed out with the arrival of Mae and Dan's first child, a boy. They named him Kenneth Claude Lynch. Throughout that year, Creed and Blanch had been talking a great deal about moving to Colorado, and Dan and Mae were starting to talk seriously about going as well. Dan was also fed up with the constant flooding. But by the end of 1909, those plans, serious or not, were put on hold. Mae didn't want to make such a drastic move with a newborn baby, and not long after Kenneth was born, Creed and Blanch announced that they were expecting another child. It was obvious to everyone that any plans of moving to Colorado were plans for the future—most certainly a few years away.

CHAPTER 4

1910 to 1916: Colorado Fever

JUST BEFORE THE SPRING PLANTING SEASON OF 1910, DAN HEARD OF a potentially good farming opportunity in Chase County, Kansas, near a settlement called Toledo. He and Mae announced to their families that they were going to give it a try, and soon they had their wagon packed and were headed to Kansas. A letter from Mae arrived in a few days, saying that they had found a house to rent in Cottonwood Falls, Kansas, just a few miles from Toledo.

Gertie was also sending letters home, from Braymer. She had met a man from Braymer named Bennett Long. He was a farmer, and his farm was near the Hazel Dell School where she was teaching. In her next letter, she happily reported that she and Bennett were planning to be married. A few days later, another letter arrived: a wedding announcement. She and Bennett had traveled to Cottonwood Falls and were married on September 14 at Dan and Mae's home.

In October 1910, Blanch gave birth to Creed's tenth child and her fifth. They named her Ruby Estle Winfrey. Ruby was thirty years younger than her half-sister Mae, and sixteen years younger than Mary Ethel. By the time Ruby was born, Mae and Dan had been married for four years, and Ruby was almost a year younger than her nephew Kenneth.

Dan and Mae did not stay in Kansas long. In the spring of 1911, they moved back to Eugene. The farming conditions in Kansas were disappointing once more, and Mae was expecting again. They wanted to be home for the birth of their second baby. Mary Ethel was thrilled to have Mae close again—she had missed her terribly. Mae was not just her sister; she was her best friend. They could spend hours together talking about everything, and Mary Ethel depended on Mae for advice, encouragement, and support. But the best times were when Mae would braid and style Mary Ethel's long hair and tell her how pretty she was.

The family received letters from Claude and Harley throughout 1911. Mail from Colorado came to Carrollton by train. Once a letter could be taken to a train station, it would arrive in Carrollton in just a few days. Claude had found some available acreage he liked in Baca County, near Two Buttes, Colorado, and his letters sounded encouraging. But Harley didn't stay in Colorado for long. He decided to leave the claim-staking to Claude, and he returned to the Oklahoma wheat harvest.

Just before Christmas, Creed and Blanch received a letter from Claude telling them that Harley had not returned to Colorado after the wheat harvest. It appeared that he was planning to stay in Oklahoma for a while longer. Claude also told them that he had been to the land office in Springfield, Colorado, and had filed his claim for 320 acres in Baca County. He explained that it would take about a year to get the legal ownership papers, but he was excited about being a bona fide homesteader.

The next letter they received was from Harley. It explained why he was staying in Oklahoma: he had met and fallen in love with Viola Simmons. He and Viola would soon be married.

Mae and Dan had their second child near the end of 1911. He was two years younger than Kenneth, and they called him Nugent.

By that spring, Mary Ethel was spending her days helping her mother and father work the farm. She hadn't seen Archie in a long time. Since she was no longer attending school, there was little opportunity to see him, and he was becoming a distant, but not forgotten, memory. Otto was working on John and Ella Lynch's farm, and occasionally Mary Ethel would take the horse and buggy over to the Lynch farm to visit with Mae and take Otto his lunch. It was on one of those trips that she saw Leander Bailey, whom everyone called Lee, for the first time.

Lee was a friend of Dan's and had also been working on the Lynch farm for a while. Mary Ethel knew about him because Otto had spoken of him often. After visiting with Mae, Mary Ethel drove the buggy out to the field to find Otto. Otto and Lee were working in the field together, and she was caught off guard when Lee smiled at her and stopped what he was doing so that he could meet her. He was surprisingly handsome, with red hair and sparkling blue eyes. She had never been smiled at quite like that before. She drove the buggy home that day thinking of nothing but him.

Soon after Mary Ethel met Lee, the world and national news was filled with reports on the sinking of the Titanic. Everyone eagerly awaited each weekly newspaper, in anticipation of getting more information about the outcome of that tragic event. Mary Ethel was interested in the news about the Titanic, but she was too distracted by her thoughts of Lee to be too concerned.

By the summer of 1912, Harley had written that he and Viola had married in April of that year. He wrote that she was called Sis by everyone in her family. He was planning on staying in Oklahoma. Also that year, Gertie and Bennett had a baby, whom they named Mildred Irene Long. And Lee Bailey was coming to the Winfrey farm often to visit Otto.

In the fall of 1912, Mary Ethel and several other family members saw an automobile for the first time. A family well known to Creed and Blanch had driven their new Model T to the Winfrey farm. The ground was wet after a recent rain, and the car left tire marks in the ground near the house. Emil was so excited about seeing the car that as soon as it had departed, he gathered up various objects to make a border around the tire marks. He guarded that border constantly, so that the tracks would be preserved for as long as possible.

A few days later, Lee Bailey found another good reason to once again visit Otto. While he was there, he asked Creed for permission to see Mary Ethel. Creed hesitantly gave Lee permission, and the very next day, Lee came calling. Since all courting had to be chaperoned, Lee and Mary Ethel sat on the front porch, drinking lemonade and getting to know each other. It was on that first date that Lee told her all about his family. He had been born in Mountain Grove, Missouri, but his father, Willis, now lived in nearby Buchanan. His mother, Annie, had died several years earlier. He had two brothers, one older and one younger, and two sisters, one older and one younger. His younger sister's name was Lola. His older sister was also named Ethel, but she went by her middle name, Edna. He told Mary Ethel that he really liked the name Ethel, and if it was all right with her, he would like to just call her Ethel. That was perfectly fine with her.

From that point on, she began telling everyone that she preferred to go by Ethel, rather than Mary Ethel, and everyone complied. After that first date, Lee became a regular visitor at the Winfrey farm. Their dates consisted of horse-and-buggy rides, church functions, and school events.

The next year, 1913, brought more letters from Harley and Claude. Claude had built, and was living in, a dugout. Many homes on the Great Plains were what were called half-dugouts. A half-dugout was constructed by digging a large hole into the earth, usually at least twelve-by-twelve feet in length and width, and about five to six feet in depth. Short wooden walls, about two feet high, were anchored around the hole, which was covered with a slightly pitched roof. People often put narrow windows in the walls just above the ground, if they could afford the glass. The roofs were covered with tar paper, which was then covered with sod. Four or five steps were dug into the ground for an entrance, and a small room was built over the steps to enclose the entryway. This above-ground entryway room was often used as a doghouse and to store firewood. The dugouts were usually just one room—only big enough for a cook stove in the corner, a table and chairs, and a bed. The walls were dirt; the floors were usually dirt as well, although some had wooden floors. Dugouts provided warmth in the winter and were cool in the summer. Claude's was about five miles west of Two Buttes. He wrote that his corn and bean crops were doing well, and he liked it there. Harley's letters from Oklahoma were also full of good news: he and Sis had had a son in January, Joe Glendon Winfrey.

But as far as Ethel was concerned, the most exciting news came from her when she told her mother that she was in love with Lee, and he was in love with her. During the early part of 1913, Jesse Wallace, who went by Jess, had given Lee a well-paying job with the railroad. Jess was well known to the Winfrey family—he had always lived in nearby Wakenda—and as Lee's boss, he had promised to help Lee "move up the ladder" in the railroad industry. The railroad business was big business; the prospect of Lee moving up in it added even more excitement to Ethel's news.

But the person whom Ethel was most anxious to tell about Lee was Mae. She couldn't wait to tell her half-sister that she was in love. When she did, Mae was happy for her. It was during this conversation that Mae told Ethel that Dan had heard of a good farming opportunity in Arkansas, and they might be moving soon. Ethel was disappointed, but she understood. It seemed as though everyone was looking for an opportunity to leave Carroll County.

Late in December, good news arrived from Claude. He had received his land patent documentation on December 9, 1913—he *officially* owned 320 acres in Baca County, Colorado.

It wasn't long after Lee started his job with the railroad that he asked Ethel to marry him. The future looked bright, he was excited about the prospect of moving up with the railroad, and for the first time, he had a regular paycheck coming in. Ethel couldn't have been happier; she said yes almost before Lee had finished his proposal. After her quick acceptance, Lee had another surprise for her. The railroad men wanted him to relocate to Milan, Missouri, and they wanted him to move there soon. He and Ethel would need to get married and move to Milan as soon as possible. The news about Milan was more than a surprise to Ethel—it was a shock. Milan was eighty-five miles from Eugene. She had never been that far away from her family.

Ethel couldn't wait to tell her mother that Lee wanted to marry her, but when she did, Blanch's response was a surprise. Blanch was not as happy for her as Ethel had expected her to be. In fact, Blanch told her that if Lee asked her father for permission to marry her, Creed may say no. Ethel was surprised again when Otto, the person who had known

Lee the longest, expressed his own opposition to the marriage. She didn't know why, and the truth was, she didn't really care—it didn't matter. They were in love, and there was no doubt—there was nothing but happiness ahead of them. Of course, the person Ethel wanted most to talk to about marrying Lee was Mae. But shortly before Lee proposed, Mae and Dan had moved to Piggott, Arkansas, in another attempt to find a better farming situation. This time, the only way Ethel could confide in Mae was in a letter.

Ethel had known Jess Wallace most of her life, and she and Lee were invited to supper by Jess's wife, Elsie, quite often. Elsie and Jess were supportive of Ethel and Lee's courtship, and Jess encouraged them to get married as soon as possible. With that encouragement, and with the knowledge that Creed would probably not give his blessing to their marriage, they decided to elope. On Ethel's first visit to meet Lee's dad, Willis, in Buchanan, they applied for their marriage license, and on Saturday, January 3, 1914, after an afternoon with—and with the help of—Jess and Elsie, they eloped. They were married by a justice of the peace. Jess signed as a witness.

Their elopement was exciting, daring, and exhilarating. Immediately following their marriage, they headed to the Winfrey farm to tell everyone that they were now Mr. and Mrs. Leander Roseling Bailey. Creed congratulated them and welcomed Lee to the family, but Ethel knew he was not particularly happy. Blanch told Ethel that she was happy for them and helped her pack her things. Ethel had asked her grandmother Nancy, who was now living in Carrollton, if she and Lee could spend their first night together at her house, and her grandmother had said yes. It was the first night Ethel had ever spent away from her family. She was nineteen; Lee was eighteen.

The day after their elopement, Lee and Ethel went to Milan, where they found a house to rent and bought furniture for their home. For both of them, the preparation for a new beginning was an exciting time. Ethel was scared, but she was very much in love, and she knew their future was bright.

That bright future became a quick reality. Shortly after they had gotten settled in Milan, she realized that she was expecting. The timing was perfect, and there was nothing but happiness for them both. They would be a family of three by early November.

During that summer, the important national and world news was reports on what was being called the Great War. Newspapers reported that President Woodrow Wilson was intent on the United States staying out of the war. The news was interesting, but it had little effect on Ethel and Lee's daily life. To them, it was just "something that was going on—over there."

Toward the end of that summer, Ethel received a letter from her mother. Mae and Dan's little Nugent had died of what they called "summer complaint," a term used for conditions of uncontrollable diarrhea occurring in infants and babies during the summer months. It was difficult to keep food refrigerated during the hot summer days, and it was thought that young children got dysentery from spoiled milk. Nugent was two and a half years old. This news made Ethel long to be home. She hated being so far from her family during this time of extreme sadness.

Exactly ten months after their marriage, Ethel went into labor. It was difficult and long. Lee was able to find a midwife to come to their home, and happily, Ethel gave birth, on November 1, 1914, to a baby daughter with red hair. They named her Inez Bailey. She was a healthy, happy baby, despite the long labor, and because Ethel had helped her mother care for Ruby, she was completely confident that she could take care of a baby of her own. Inez was the icing on the cake of their new beginning. For three days, they reveled in the excitement of their first child.

On the morning of November 5, the day Inez turned four days old, Ethel awoke to a cold baby whom she was unable to arouse. Because money was tight, they had been unable to buy a bassinet for Inez; she was kept in the bed between them each night. Amid the panic, Lee left for help, returning with a doctor who immediately summoned the coroner. The cause of Inez's death was not known, but Lee and Ethel both feared that one of them had rolled over and smothered her during the night. Whatever the cause, the alarming realization was that Inez was dead. The cause of death listed by the coroner on her death certificate was "baby colic," with "cramps and indigestion," but Lee and Ethel both knew that that was not true. Each felt that one of them was to blame, but they did not know who. Inez was gone. Not a single member of either of their families had ever even seen her. Suddenly their bright new beginning had a heavy cloud of darkness over it.

They went together to the Wilhite Cemetery in Milan to bury their baby. Now, long days of completely unexpected sadness and grief lay ahead of them. Ethel depended on her faith to help get her through her grief, quoting a verse from Psalms over and over to herself: *"God is our refuge and strength, a very present help in trouble"* (Psalms 46:1).

By the beginning of 1915, Lee had been working for the railroad for well over a year, but no promotion had yet been offered. Because of this, he and Ethel decided to leave Milan and move back to Carrollton. There was always farm work to be done, and Lee knew how badly Ethel missed her family.

Not long after their move back, Mae sent word that she and Dan had a new baby daughter, Mary Lorene. But Mae's letter said that they were struggling in Piggott, and they too were planning to return to Carrollton soon. Mary was two months old when Mae and Dan moved home. They arrived with news that they had decided to follow Claude's lead and go to Colorado. Dan would go to Colorado first, and Mae and the children would follow once Dan had things ready for them. Dan didn't hesitate to ask Lee if he was interested in going to Colorado with him. Soon the two of them were making plans.

With a mixture of emotions, Ethel accepted the fact that Lee wanted to give Colorado a try. Her mother and father had also been hit with "Colorado fever," and Ethel knew there was no stopping any of them now. So she began making plans as well.

Then, in July, she realized that she was expecting again. She and Lee were happy, but worried. They had to do everything right this time, which meant that she could not make the trip to Colorado until after the baby was born. Now the decisions were easy: Dan and Lee would take wagons to Colorado. When they had made arrangements there, Mae and the children would go out by train. Ethel would stay in

Carrollton until after the baby was born. She too would go to Colorado by train, when the baby was old enough to travel.

The next family news was from Claude. He wrote to say that he had left Colorado and was in Oklahoma for the 1915 wheat harvest. He was staying in Rosston, Oklahoma, near where Harley was. He would be staying there the entire summer.

The national news was now beginning to hint that the United States may become involved in the Great War. On May 7, 1915, a German submarine torpedoed the RMS *Lusitania*, and the British luxury liner sank within eighteen minutes. Many Americans were on that ship; many were killed. Newspapers across the country reported that most Americans considered the sinking of the *Lusitania* as an act of war.

After careful consideration, Creed and Blanch made the difficult decision that they too would be going to Colorado. The decision was difficult because Creed, at the age of fifty-eight, was no longer a young man. Even though the words were probably not spoken, they both knew that this move would be a permanent one—they would need to take almost everything they owned. The first thing they did was leave the farm in Eugene and move into a rented house in Carrollton, bringing with them all the things they would be taking to Colorado. They planned to move the livestock to Colorado as well, but the stock would stay on the farm until the actual move date. Plans were made to charter railroad cars, in which they would move everything. The packing was not easy. Wooden crates had to be built, and everything breakable had to be packed in sawdust.

By August, Dan and Lee were ready to go, their wagons packed with enough supplies to last several months. The terribly difficult good-byes were said. It was an extremely hard time for both Mae and Ethel, but it helped that they had each other. When Lee left, Ethel moved into the rented house in Carrollton with her parents and stored most of their things there.

Not long after Dan and Lee left for Colorado, word arrived from Claude: he had married Erma Borum, whom he had met in Rosston. Claude and Erma were planning to stay in Rosston a little while longer, but they would be moving out to his homestead near Two Buttes before the start of the cold weather. Claude and Erma's first child, Irene, eventually wrote the story of her life on the Great Plains of Colorado. In her book, *Irene and Levi, Our Journey Through Life*, she wrote about her mother, Erma, leaving her home in Rosston to go with her father, Claude, to the Colorado prairie:

> *I can see my grandmother and grandfather standing there to say farewell to my mother and not knowing they might be seeing her for the last time. My dad did promise my grandmother that he would bring her back to visit as often as he could. I have heard my dad mention that grandmother never cared too much for him, because he took her baby so far away from them.... My mother followed her husband convinced that her rightful place was by his side, regardless of the strong ties pulling her from the home she had known and loved.... Erma Borum was a schoolteacher and she left her friends and family and moved to Colorado to a very hard and more difficult life than she had been used to.... In those days a woman's life on the prairie consisted of herding J.J. cattle out of wheat fields, washing clothes on the wash-board, hauling water with a wagon and team several miles a couple of times a week and picking cow chips to keep the cook stove burning. Then as her family came along, the work became much harder.*

Other news from Oklahoma that year came from Harley and Sis. They had their second son in 1915, Wayne W. Winfrey.

It was a long time before anyone in Carrollton heard from Lee or Dan, but finally a letter came. They had made it to Colorado and had found good land upon which to stake claims. The land was near a small town called Kim, about sixty-five miles southwest of Claude's claim near Two Buttes. Kim consisted primarily of a general store and a post office. Dan was the one who wrote, saying that he and Lee were living out of their wagons and were preparing to build a dugout. They were trying to get things ready for Mae and the children before it got cold. The news from Dan was especially encouraging for Creed. Once he heard that good land was available, he arranged for his charter of two railroad cars to take everything he owned to Colorado. The date for the move was set for Monday, March 13, 1916.

Ethel spent that winter getting ready for the new baby, due sometime around the middle of March, and planning what she would take to Colorado on the train. Mae and Blanch were also getting ready for the move. By the end of February, everyone knew that it was probably just a matter of weeks before Mae, Kenneth, and Mary would be leaving. Blanch had decided that if Ethel's baby was not born before the scheduled move date, she and Ruby would stay in Carrollton with Ethel until the baby was born.

Then, sometime around the first of March, Mae got a letter from Dan. The winter had been extremely hard in Colorado, and he was not staying. His plans were to go to Oklahoma. He would send for Mae, Kenneth, and Mary just as soon as he found a job and a place to live. Ethel got a letter from Lee in which he expressed his disappointment that Dan was not staying in Colorado. He was definitely going to stay. He said that Harley was returning to Colorado soon, where he would find a place to stake a claim and be there to help Creed and Blanch "prove up" their claim. It was Lee's understanding that Harley's wife, Sis, was staying in Oklahoma with their two sons.

Lee told Ethel to send a telegram to the telegraph office in Kim to let him know when she would be coming to Colorado. He would go to Kim every day to check for her telegram. Within a matter of days, Mae received a telegram from Dan telling her to come to Oklahoma. Mae, Kenneth, and Mary left almost immediately.

On March 10, two railroad cars were pulled to a side track at the station in Carrollton, and Creed, Emil, and Otto began loading them. Their wagon and buggy, beds, tables, chairs, blankets, clothing, tools, canned food, gallons of kerosene and coal oil, lanterns, reams of cloth for making clothes, and the Winfrey treadle sewing machine were loaded on the train. Once the furniture was loaded, Blanch, Ruby, and Ethel moved into the Carrollton home of Arthur and Rose Winfrey. Arthur was Ethel's first cousin, the son of Creed's brother James.

Of the ten Winfrey children, four were not planning to go to Colorado. Sometime in 1915, Otto had begun a courtship with Edna Stewart, which quickly became serious; on January 30, 1916, they married. Otto was farming the Winfrey farm, and because of Edna, he was planning to stay there forever. Sue and Nancy were also still living on the Winfrey farm. Neither was married, and both were working at the Chapman & Dewey Box Factory. At least for the time being, they were planning on staying in Eugene.

March 13 was approaching quickly. Ethel knew that Blanch was hoping the baby would come in time for her and Ruby to go to Colorado with Creed and Emil. It almost happened that way, but didn't. Early on Monday morning, March 13, Creed and fourteen-year-old Emil boarded the train and left for Colorado. Emil was assigned the job of riding in the stock car with the horses, cows, pigs, and chickens, to ensure that the stock made the trip successfully.

Then, just hours after Creed and Emil's train pulled away from the Carrollton station, Ethel went into labor. Her labor was once again long, but a doctor arrived, and Blanch was there as well. Before the day ended, Ethel had given birth to a healthy, red-haired baby boy. He was born in the home of Arthur and Rose Winfrey, on the same day that Creed and Emil left for Colorado. Ethel named him just what she and Lee had planned, were it a boy: Robert Leonard Bailey.

As soon as Blanch knew that the baby was healthy and Ethel was fine, she purchased her train tickets. Within two days of Robert's birth, Blanch and six-year-old Ruby were on their way to Colorado. Arthur and Rose wanted Ethel to stay with them until she was confident that she could make the trip to Colorado with Robert, but Ethel was fighting a sudden feeling of urgency to get to Colorado to be with Lee. Robert was only a week old when she decided that she could do it.

She sent a telegram to Lee to tell him her plans. She would be leaving on the afternoon of Monday, March 27, and she would arrive in Lamar, Colorado, early Tuesday morning, March 28. Lee's return telegram told her to wait at the Lamar station. He would get there as soon as he could that Tuesday. Robert would be two weeks and one day old when she arrived.

It seemed to Ethel that March 27 would never arrive. She had been preparing for her train trip with her newborn baby for a long time, and she was ready to go. Rose had been helping her prepare food to carry on the train. She would be traveling on the Atchison, Topeka and Santa Fe Railway train called the California Limited. It would be a fifteen-hour trip, but she had a ticket for a Pullman sleeping car, and there would be multiple stops along the way. She knew she could do it, and she absolutely could not wait to get to Colorado to be with Lee.

Finally, the departure date arrived, and Arthur and Rose took her to the train station. She had lots of jelly sandwiches, lots of Rose's fried pies, clean diapers for Robert, and her Bible packed in the bag she would carry with her on the train. Her large bags and two large trunks were loaded into the baggage compartment. With Robert in her arms, she stepped onto the train. As she turned to wave good-bye to Arthur and Rose, she had to fight the sudden sadness that came over her. She was leaving the place where she had grown up, the place she loved, and a realization came to her with a jolt: all of a sudden, she was sure she would never return. She was twenty-one years old.

CHAPTER 5

1916: The Great Plains of Colorado—Another New Start

THE TRAIN WAS BOTH COMFORTABLE AND EXCITING. THIS WAS THE first time Ethel had ever been on a train, and the California Limited was beautiful. Lee had told her about the Pullman cars, but she had to see it to believe it. She had a couch-like seat, which faced another seat just like it. The seats of the two couches pulled out and together, which enabled the seatbacks to slide down to make a bed. A curtain could be pulled for privacy. It was grand!

The second stop was in Kansas City, and while there, the porters prepared the train for the nighttime journey across Kansas. As the train pulled out of the Kansas City station, Ethel settled in for a long night, happy that she would see Lee the next day.

As she surrounded Robert with pillows, the motion of the train put him to sleep quickly, and soon she was sleeping as well. However, at some point along the way, she awoke shaking, in a state of complete fear. She had dreamed that Robert was gone, and she was frantically searching for him. She had broken into a cold sweat, and she was experiencing the same feeling of panic that she'd had with Inez. When she was fully awake, she realized that he was still right beside her, and he was fine. After that, she refused to let herself go to sleep again.

When the porter came to make the sleeping berths back into couches, he told her they were getting close to Garden City. Garden City was just two stops away from Lamar. They would be there soon.

The train arrived in Lamar around eight o'clock in the morning. Ethel knew that Lee could not be there until later in the day. It would take him two days to get from his camp near Kim to Lamar, so she found a comfortable place in the Lamar station to wait. But shortly after noon, it wasn't Lee who walked into the train station. It was her brother Harley. She was happy to see Harley but terribly disappointed that it wasn't Lee who had come for her. Harley, seeing her disappointment, quickly explained that various job opportunities were being reported in Trinidad, Colorado, so Lee had gone there to try to find work. Trinidad was seventy miles west of Kim, and a two-day wagon trip from Harley and Lee's campsite. It was a thriving city with a population of eleven thousand in 1916. It was thriving because it was a primary supply and transportation center for the Colorado cattle and coal mining industries. Trinidad was the closest large city to Kim, and it offered the best possibility to find work. Harley made sure Ethel understood that Lee had gone to Trinidad only after Harley had assured him that he would go to Lamar to get her and the baby.

Ethel knew that life in Colorado would be hard—she had never imagined it would be easy—but this was an especially unexpected and difficult start. The two-day wagon trip from Lamar to Harley's camp was long, rough, and tiresome, but she needed that time to get acclimated, and she was grateful to have it. Harley tried to tell her everything he could about what was ahead. He told her that he would be in Colorado for only a few more days—just as soon as the major work on Creed and Blanch's claim was done, he would be leaving for home in Oklahoma.

He also told her that after Dan left for Oklahoma, Lee had decided that he and Ethel would also go to the Oklahoma wheat fields. It cost money to build a dugout, and the fastest way to get that money was to go to the wheat harvest. But money was also needed to get to Oklahoma, so Lee had gone to Trinidad to make that money. Then Harley confirmed what Ethel was beginning to fear: she and the baby would have to stay at Harley's camp until Lee returned, or until Creed and Blanch's dugout was complete.

Even though Harley had tried to prepare her, Ethel was still amazed to see that his camp consisted of a two-foot-deep hole in the ground, covered with his wagon cover. She tried to hide her anxiety, but Harley felt her apprehension. He quickly told her that he had decided not to go home until Lee returned. Then they would all go to Oklahoma together. He assured her that she and the baby would be fine under the wagon cover, and that he would sleep under the wagon nearby. She pretended to be brave, but the only thing that gave her any consolation was the knowledge that her mother and father were not too far away.

This certainly wasn't how she had imagined it would be. She had hoped that things would be somewhat ready for her when she arrived, but she had hoped for too much. She was, however, very grateful that they would be going to Creed and Blanch's claim site the next day. Harley had said that Claude and Erma would be there too. Claude was also helping Creed and Blanch build their dugout, their barn, and their fences—and there was still plenty of work to do. Claude's claim, near Two Buttes, was a two-day wagon trip from Creed and Blanch's claim, so Claude and Erma were camping at Creed and Blanch's to help them "prove up" their claim. Harley's announcement that she would get to see her family the next morning was the best thing Ethel had heard the entire day.

When they had first arrived at Harley's camp, she immediately noticed that the things she had sent to Colorado with Lee had been left with Harley. She was especially glad to see her big washtub. She would be able to bathe Robert with that tub and keep him in clean diapers.

That first night in Harley's camp brought her to a realization: she was at an impasse in her life. She was in Colorado, and there was absolutely no going back. She made up her mind that night that if this was what Lee wanted, she could and would do it. It would be hard, but she would do whatever was required. Once again, she depended on her faith to strengthen her, finding comfort in her favorite Bible verse: *"I can do all things through Christ which strengtheneth me"* (Philippians 4:13). As she blew out her lamp, she thought about beautiful Carrollton—at that point, it felt as if it had been an eternity since she had said good-bye to Arthur and Rose at the train station. Her last thought that night was of how thankful she was that Rose had insisted on packing all that food into her bag. She was not going to sleep hungry, only because of Rose.

Harley and Ethel, with Robert in tow, set off for Creed and Blanch's claim early the next morning. The claim site was about two and a half miles from Harley's camp and about nine miles from Kim. This was an exceptionally good claim, because their 320 acres were bordered on the north by the much-used road that ran between Kim and Springfield, Colorado. As they traveled on the rough wagon road, Ethel was amazed at how flat and barren the country was. Unlike the rolling, tree-covered hills of Missouri, there were no hills, and there were no trees.

She was also fighting the feeling of isolation that had been encumbering her since she and Harley left Lamar. When traveling through Carroll County, the roads led past neighbor after neighbor. Here in Colorado, there appeared to be no one—no neighbors, no people. But she sat up straight and smiled in an effort to hide her concerns from Harley. It was best to think about the oncoming spring, and how light the air was, and how wonderful it smelled. She asked Harley if he loved it here. Harley said no.

A joyous reunion took place when they arrived at Creed and Blanch's claim site. Seeing her mother, father, Claude, Emil, and Ruby helped lift Ethel's sadness over Lee's absence, and as soon as she saw Claude's wife, Erma, she knew they were going to become the best of friends. They all spent the day working on Creed and Blanch's claim, while Ruby watched after Robert. Ethel was sure she didn't have to tell her mother how disappointed she was that Lee was not there, but Blanch let her know that it was good if Lee had found work in Trinidad. The best place to make money was in the Oklahoma wheat harvest, but it cost money to get there. Blanch also told Ethel that she and Creed had decided that Emil would also be going with them to the wheat fields. They had received word from Dan and Mae; Dan had suggested that they all come to where he and Mae were living. He said there was plenty of work, and the pay was good. So it was decided that day: when Lee returned from Trinidad, Harley, Emil, Lee, Ethel, and Robert would leave for the wheat fields.

It was on that first day of work on Creed and Blanch's claim that Ethel was so surprised to learn that water was not readily available. Creed and Harley hauled water from a farmer's well on an adjoining claim, and Harley only took enough to his camp to drink. This was worrisome. She had a lot of diapers to wash. Blanch apparently could read her mind and told her to plan on doing all her washing and bathing at their claim, emphasizing that under no circumstances could water be wasted. As Ethel went to get a drink of water that day, she thought about the farm in Eugene and wondered, in amazement, how they had taken all that water for granted, never worrying about not having enough, and never having to think about reusing water for washing and bathing. She was learning minute by minute what a new kind of life this was going to be—and so far, nothing she had learned was reassuring. But she was extremely grateful that her mother seemed happy about the move to Colorado. Blanch had left her entire family in Missouri. Her surprisingly bright outlook made Ethel think that maybe, just maybe, this was not going to be as bad as it seemed.

That first day at her parents' claim, Ethel met William Hardy Priddy, a young man who had come to Colorado to stake his own claim for 320 acres. Everyone called him Bill. The acreage Bill had chosen was just to the west of Creed and Blanch's claim and was also bordered on the north by the road between Springfield and Kim. He had moved to Colorado by himself from Wellington, Texas, and had quickly become good friends with Creed and his family.

Lee was in Trinidad for several weeks, but thanks to the telegraph office in Kim, Ethel was somewhat able to stay in contact with him. He sent word that as soon as he finished the work he was doing there, he would be back to Kim, and they could leave for Oklahoma. There was a lot to do while they waited. Creed was paying to store their possessions and board their stock in the town of Las Animas, so they were anxious to get their dugout, barns, and fences built. It was extremely challenging work, but Ethel could see that they were making progress. She was especially anxious for their dugout to be finished—once it was done, she and Robert would be able to quit camping with Harley. She was looking forward to that. Living in Harley's camp with a baby was difficult. Each day seemed to present another new obstacle.

During Ethel's first week on the prairie, they all learned about a problem they would most likely have to deal with at all times: the problem of open-range ranching. Herds of cattle were allowed to roam the open ranges, and the day that several cows ran through Creed's claim, they learned that barbed-wire fences would not keep the cattle out of their crops. Even though Claude and Erma had warned them about this possible problem, it was still a surprise to everyone. None of the dryland farming articles had mentioned this important difficulty. The cattle were all branded with the JJ Cattle brand. The JJ Cattle Ranch was in Colorado, not far away, and their cattle seemed to be everywhere.

Lee returned to Kim six weeks after Ethel arrived in Colorado. By then, Robert was two months old, and Ethel and Robert had been living with Creed and Blanch for about a week. Ethel could not remember ever being as happy as she was the day Lee returned. His arrival brought her a sense of peace and hopefulness—feelings she had not had since leaving Missouri. Lee too was extremely happy to be back, and excited to see his new son for the first time. He arrived with gifts for Ethel and Robert.

He was also excited about leaving for Oklahoma. There was money to be made there, and the sooner they got there, the better. They didn't waste any time. Almost immediately after Lee arrived, they loaded up their wagons, and Ethel, Lee, and their two-month-old baby followed Harley and Emil to Oklahoma. Harley was planning to help them find jobs and a place to live near Dan and Mae, and to work a few days in the wheat fields before he headed home to Sis and his sons.

It took them eight long days to reach Dan and Mae's. By the time they arrived, Dan had made arrangements. The man he was working for had assured him that there would be work for the men, and he'd told Dan that they could camp out of their wagons close to his house. They quickly set up their camps, and the men began working immediately. They were up early each morning and out in the fields ready to start working by daybreak. While the men worked in the fields, Ethel and Mae cooked, washed, and watched over Kenneth, Mary, and Robert. Dan and Mae were renting a house, so Ethel spent her days there, but at the end of each day, she, Lee, and Robert, along with Harley and Emil, would go to their wagons to sleep.

On one particular morning in late May 1916, about a week after their arrival in Oklahoma, Ethel noticed dark clouds far out on the western horizon. The land was so flat that you could see for miles and miles. She began preparing to spend the day with Mae, but when she looked at the sky a few minutes later, she saw that those dark clouds were now much closer and much darker. The wind was starting to blow. She worried about Lee, Harley, and Emil out in the fields and decided that she would not go to Mae's until the skies had cleared. However, before she could even think about what to do next, she saw Harley and Emil running for their camp. The wind was picking up such force that it was beginning to be difficult to stay standing.

Harley was yelling to anyone who could hear, "Cyclone, take cover!" He ran to Ethel and grabbed Robert out of her arms, and she and Emil followed him to the nearby house, barely able to walk against the driving wind.

Once they had made it inside, Ethel began screaming to Harley, asking if he knew where Lee was. Harley admitted that he did not know how far away Lee had been working that morning, as he pulled her away from the window. It was several minutes—which seemed like hours to Ethel—before they heard the door of the house open. Lee ran in. He'd had a difficult time finding the house, but he had made it!

The tornado was fierce. It tossed their wagons over easily, and all their possessions were blown away. But worst of all, they feared that their horses, which were tied to the wagons, would be strangled by the ropes around their necks. Harley was sure they would be killed. As some of the windows of the house started breaking, they all thought that the house could not possibly stand.

The wind finally stopped as abruptly as it had started, and thankfully, the house had not fallen. They immediately began attending to the horses and trying to find any of their things that could be salvaged. Fortunately, their horses had survived, but almost everything they owned was gone. But those losses didn't matter, they were just happy to be alive, and once they learned that Mae, Dan, Kenneth, and Mary were all okay, nothing else was important.

Lee assured Ethel that everything was going to be fine, as he headed out to find a house that he had heard might be for rent. When he returned, he brought good news: he had located the house and rented it. They could move in right away. It was a somewhat furnished parsonage, owned by a local church that did not have a pastor. The church members were happy to rent it to him—for practically nothing. Ethel was extremely relieved to have a place to live. She, Lee, and Emil moved what few things they had left after the tornado into the parsonage.

Harley began repairing his wagon. The storm had made him anxious to see his family, and as soon as his wagon was repaired and his horse had recovered, he left for home.

Lee, Ethel, Robert, and Emil lived in the parsonage until the end of the wheat harvest. The tornado had cost them a great deal, but when the work ended in Oklahoma, they had the money they needed to get back to Colorado, build their dugout, and make it through the oncoming winter.

Mae and Dan also left Oklahoma as soon as the harvest work was done. Dan had decided to look into the coal-mining business, and Trinidad was the place to find a mining job. Ethel was heartbroken that Mae and Dan would not be going back to Kim with them, but Dan was extremely ambitious, and the newspapers were reporting much-improved conditions for coal miners. They all left Oklahoma at the same time, with Mae promising that she would write just as soon as she knew where they would be living.

A great deal had happened by the time Lee, Ethel, Emil, and Robert got back to the Kim area. Creed and Blanch were now fairly well established, and Ethel's twin sisters, Nancy and Sue, had, at the urging of their mother, moved to Colorado. Creed and Blanch had enlarged their dugout to make room for two more. But Sue did not live with her parents for long. It appears that it was love at first sight for Sue and Bill Priddy, because on August 20, 1916, they went to Clayton, New Mexico, where they were married. Sue was twenty years old.

With Creed and Blanch's claim site almost complete, Creed and Emil were able to help Lee and Ethel build their dugout. Lee decided on an available 320-acre plot of land about two and a half miles northwest of Blanch and Creed's claim, near where Harley's camp had been. Lee and Ethel went immediately to the Lamar land office to file their claim. The home they built was a twelve-by-sixteen-foot hole in the ground, dug about six feet deep. The roof was two feet above ground, and they had enough money to put two windows in the walls just above the ground. It was a one-room dugout, with a four-plate wood-burning cook stove in one corner. A curtain hung over another corner, behind which was a small table with a wash basin. All of their bathing would be done behind the curtain. Their bed was the pallet from their wagon on the dirt floor. A large wooden box, brought from Oklahoma, was made into a crib for Robert.

When the dugout was finished, Creed and Emil helped Lee build a small barn for his horse, a chicken coop, and a pigpen, and he and Ethel bought a few chickens and two pigs from Creed. When all the work was done, Ethel was hopeful that this would be the beginning of a longed-for security—it had been a long time since she had felt secure.

The coming of fall meant that the men would soon be going to the cedars. The people living on the Great Plains referred to the place where the men went for wood as "the cedars." They would usually travel in groups and camp out, while they filled their wagons with what they hoped would be enough scrub cedarwood to last through the winter. The 1916 trek to the cedars would be the first for Creed, Emil, Lee, and Bill Priddy; Claude had been before, and he told them to expect to be gone for possibly up to three weeks. The timing of this year's trip was going to be good, because Erma, Claude's wife, was expecting their first child, and they would be back long before her anticipated delivery date.

However, the trip ended up having to be delayed. On September 1, Erma went into premature labor and delivered, in Claude's and her dugout, a tiny baby girl. The baby was so small that she was not expected to live. They named her Irene Gertrude Winfrey. Irene later described her start in life in her book, *Irene and Levi, Our Journey Through Life*:

> *I was told that I was a very tiny baby. The doctor said I probably weighed around one and one-half pounds. No scales were available to find out for sure. The folks said they could hold me in the palm of their hand. Doctor Verity was a good doctor, but very rough, I was told. He was well known for miles around, but never had any sympathy for his patients.*
>
> *Well, the next thing was how to keep me alive, being such a small baby. He asked for a shoebox (man sized). They sewed outing flannel on the sides and a small pillow with a flannel slip on it was put in the box. The water was warmed and put in a hot water bottle and placed on the bottom of the shoebox. The water was tested by putting their elbow into it, so that it would not burn me. This was done every few hours, night and day for six long weeks. What a time they went thru to give me a start in life. They were so tired from sitting up with me and changing the water in the bottle. Think how often they had to warm the water.*

No one was more surprised than Dr. Verity that Irene did not die. When Claude was sure that she would survive, the men left for the cedars. Ethel and Robert stayed with Erma and Irene while they were gone. Irene was five and a half months younger than Robert.

Ethel was extremely happy to be close to her family—they needed each other, and she could not imagine being on that prairie without them. When the men returned with plenty of wood, Ethel was thankful that she and Lee were finally self-sufficient. Now they could officially begin their new life together in Colorado.

Winter was coming, and they were ready. That October, when Robert turned seven months old, she realized that she had a surprise for Lee: she was expecting another baby.

CHAPTER 6

1917 to 1918: America Enters World War I

THAT FIRST WINTER ON THE COLORADO PRAIRIE WAS FULL OF DIFFICULT learning experiences. The dugout was warm and made Ethel feel safe, but it seemed that the main objective each day was to just survive. There were long days of staying in the dugout, listening to the howling wind, while they waited out sudden snowstorms.

Every time weather permitted, Lee would haul water from a nearby farmer's well, and Ethel would attempt to do laundry. Laundry days on the prairie were the most difficult work days. Water had to be carried into the dugout and warmed on the stove. Then buckets of hot water would be carried out to the washtub outside. More cold water had to be put in the rinse tub. A scrub board was used to scrub each piece of clothing, using lye soap. Then each piece was rinsed and wrung out by hand. That first year, the clothes were hung over the fences to dry if the weather was good. If not, the laundry was hung all over the dugout. After the laundry was dry, each piece had to be ironed. The iron was heated on the cook stove, and Ethel used their table as an ironing board.

To help break the winter monotony Lee made frequent trips to Kim for mail and copies of the newspaper the *Dry Land Record*. The *Dry Land Record* was published in Springfield, Colorado, fifty-two miles east of Kim, so it was considered the local paper. Lee could also get basic supplies at the general merchandise store in Kim. On one of Lee's trips to Kim early that year, he returned with a letter from Mae. Ethel opened and read it eagerly. Mae said that she and Dan were living in the coal-mining town of Primero, Colorado. Dan was mining coal for the Colorado Fuel and Iron Company. The Primero Mine was about fifteen miles west of Trinidad. Kenneth had started school at the Primero school. Mae was happy to say that the CF&I Company provided good housing, good schools, and a well-stocked general store for the coal miners and their families. She told Ethel not to worry about them. There had been two major mining accidents at the Primero Mine, but because of that, the company was making the mining industry much safer. Ethel had been worried about Mae since she had last seen her in Oklahoma. Mae's letter was like a ray of warm sunlight on a cold and dark day.

Ethel was happy to stay in the dugout that winter, caring for Robert and preparing for the new baby, but she was always thankful when the weather provided an opportunity to visit her mother and father. There seemed to constantly be family visiting Creed and Blanch's claim site, while the Winfrey women made and mended clothes on the Winfrey treadle sewing machine. Blanch had brought reams of cloth from Carrollton. There was cloth available for dresses for the women and girls and pants and shirts for the men and boys. The women and girls of the prairie always wore dresses, which were hemmed at their ankles. It was fun to see the family and share the sewing machine.

In early January, the weather cleared, and Lee saw a chance to go to Trinidad for supplies. Ethel was glad that he could go. She was aware of how difficult those long days in the dugout during the cold weather were for him. He needed a break. Lee told her that in addition to getting supplies, he thought he would also look for some short-term work while he was there. He needed to do something productive while they were waiting for spring to start planting their crops. He told her that he had made arrangements for the wife of their closest neighbor to check on her each day while he was gone. Ethel could tell there was a possibility that he could be gone for quite a while—he had filled an extra barrel full of water. Ethel was in the fourth month of her pregnancy.

The day Lee left for Trinidad, the neighbor came to check on her, just as she had promised. Ethel was doing fine and told the woman that she only needed to check on her every other day—after all, they lived a mile apart. It was on the third day after Lee's departure that Ethel picked Robert up and suddenly felt an unusual pressure. Much to her astonishment, she was bleeding. She put Robert in his crib and lay down, praying that the neighbor would come as promised, and knowing that there was not going to be a new baby after all.

Thankfully, it wasn't long before she heard the neighbor knock. The woman stayed with her and Robert until Ethel had recovered. Ethel paid her the agreed-upon price for watching after her: one pig.

When Lee returned, he was extremely saddened by the news of the miscarriage. Once again, their new life had been beset by a rough beginning. But they made it through their first long Colorado winter.

In March, Robert turned one. Lee was making plans to build fences, and they were anxiously awaiting the time to start planting corn and beans, when newspapers began reporting that Germany had resumed submarine warfare in the Atlantic. Seven US merchant ships had been sunk. President Wilson, despite his prior determination to stay out of the Great War, was now calling for war on Germany, which Congress declared on April 6, 1917. The American entry into World War I was quickly followed by the passage of the Selective Service Act, on May 18, 1917. This act gave the president the power to draft soldiers and required all men in the United States between the ages of twenty-one and thirty to register for military service.

Conscription into military service, according to the Selective Service Act, was based on class. Men were divided into five classes, and the first draftees were drawn from Class I: unmarried registrants with no dependents, or married registrants with an independent spouse and/or one or more dependent children over the age of sixteen, with sufficient family income if drafted. On June 5, 1917, Harley, Lee, and Bill Priddy went to the post office that had recently opened in Buster, Colorado, to register for the draft. Harley's registration recorded that he was married with two children. Lee's registration stated that he had a wife and a baby. It described him as tall and slender, with blue eyes and red hair. Harley and Lee undoubtedly would have been assigned to Class IV: married registrants with a dependent spouse and/or dependent children, with insufficient family income if drafted. Bill's registration recorded that he was married with no children, which would have also, more than likely, given him a status of Class IV. Harley was twenty-eight, Lee twenty-two, and Bill twenty-six. Everyone was confident that a status of Class IV would, in all likelihood, exempt them from the draft.

Lee and Ethel built their fences and planted their corn and bean crops that spring. Thanks to an adequate rainfall, everyone's crops did well. When things were slow on the claim, Lee would go to Trinidad to find some short-term work, and he would always come home with money and plenty of news about the war and the world. He was making connections in Trinidad and seemed to always be able to find some sort of work there. After each trip, he would return full of enthusiasm about the Model Ts that were becoming more and more common on the roads of Trinidad. His excitement about the cars was infectious, and he promised Ethel that someday, they would own one.

Lee and Ethel spent the summer of 1917 just getting ready for the next winter. Each day entailed keeping the JJ cattle out of their corn and killing rattlesnakes that seemed to appear from nowhere. One day that summer, Lee and Ethel left a chicken in a box in the dugout while they went to Kim for supplies. It was their best laying hen, which had become somewhat of a pet. When they returned home, their pet chicken was dead, and a large rattlesnake was curled up in the spare horse harness they kept on the dugout floor.

Ethel didn't know which was worse, the rattlesnakes or the dirt. But at least she could do something about the rattlesnakes—she could kill them, and she was getting good at that. There was nothing she could do about the endless dirt. It was like nothing she had ever experienced in her life. By now it seemed as though the beautiful rolling, tree-covered hills of Missouri were just a dream.

By fall, they were doing pretty well—they had plenty of chickens, eggs, corn, and beans. But best of all, they had each other, and that was enough for Ethel. She was slowly adjusting to the loneliness of the prairie, but she *was* adjusting. Her life was completely centered on Lee and Robert, and she was learning to just not think about the beautiful greenness of Missouri. It was better not to think of it; her life was now in Colorado, as was almost everyone she loved. Even so, that fall, she just couldn't help but think of the apple trees on their farm in Eugene, which surely would now be laden with apples. How she missed those trees!

By the fall of 1917, two schools had been built and opened in the Kim area. One was in Kim and the other, the Prairie Star School, was five miles east of Kim on the road to Springfield. Each was a one-room school with one teacher, who taught grades first through eighth. There were usually one or two children in each class. Blanch was grateful that a school was now open that Ruby could attend. Ruby started the first grade at the Prairie Star School, which was a little over four miles from Creed and Blanch's claim site.

The winter of 1917–1918 was a little easier for Lee and Ethel than their first winter on the prairie had been. At least this time, they knew what to expect, and they were ready. That December, many family members, including Mae, Dan, Kenneth, and Mary, were able to gather at Blanch and Creed's for Christmas. It wasn't a Christmas like they had always had in Missouri, but many of them were together, and that was what counted. Dan was still working for the Colorado Fuel and Iron Company, and he told them that the company was moving him to the Cameron Mine soon. The Cameron Mine was north of Trinidad in Huerfano County, Colorado. They would be moving to the town of Walsenburg, just a few miles north of Aguilar. Dan was happy with the money he was making with the CF&I Company, and he was planning to continue working for them—at least for a while.

The year 1918 was an eventful one for the Winfreys, and for the world. Spring once again brought good rainfall; if they managed to keep the JJ cattle out of their wheat and corn, they had fairly good crops. Lee was finding more and more work in Trinidad, Robert turned two in March, and Claude and Erma had their second baby, a daughter named Creeda. The Winfrey family kept Dr. Verity busy. All of them depended on him very much. Even though his office was in Two Buttes, he would drive his horse and buggy miles and miles, from claim to claim, delivering babies and tending to various illnesses and injuries.

Ethel was grateful that Dr. Verity was somewhat available, because in September of that year, she realized that she was expecting again.

Then in November, the best news of all came. The entry of the United States into World War I had made a great difference in the outcome of the war, and in November, an armistice was agreed upon. The war was to end at the eleventh hour of the eleventh day of the eleventh month of 1918. The fighting in one of the bloodiest wars in history finally came to an end.

CHAPTER 7

1919: The Founding of Andrix

BECAUSE OF THE WORK LEE WAS ABLE TO FIND IN TRINIDAD, AND because the growing season of 1918 produced a good supply of corn and beans, Lee and Ethel made it through their third long and bitterly cold Colorado winter. Ethel was always surprised by the unexpected prairie blizzards. Often, they would go from mild temperatures and no snow to freezing temperatures and a complete whiteout within an hour. The dugout was warm, but the howling wind was haunting and chilling, something she dreaded each winter. Those long prairie winters made spring a much-anticipated event. By the end of March 1919, she and Lee were anxiously awaiting the warm weather, and a new baby.

That March, Robert turned three, and on April 14, 1919, Ethel went into labor, and Lee went to get Blanch. Lee and Blanch arrived back at the claim in time. Ethel gave birth in their dugout to a daughter, whom she and Lee named Jessie Orphus Bailey—perhaps after their good friend in Missouri, Jesse Wallace, and undoubtedly after Ethel's brother Otto, whose middle name was Orphus. Ethel was elated when she saw her new baby girl. She was a beautiful, healthy baby, with red hair—just like Inez. She knew for sure that this time would be different.

In May, Harley and Sis sent word that their third son, Beverly Raymond (whom they would call Ray), had been born in April. They, along with Sis's brother Beverly Simmons, would soon be on their way, to begin proving up their claim. Then in June, a dreadful letter arrived from Otto, in Missouri. His wife Edna was extremely sick, and there was little hope. Blanch and Creed immediately began preparing to go to

Carrollton, but before they could leave, Otto sent word that Edna had died on June 13. She would be buried, along with many other Winfreys, in the Wakenda Baptist Church Cemetery, near Carrollton. She and Otto had been married for less than three and a half years, and she was only twenty-three. An intestinal obstruction was listed as the cause of death on her death certificate. Creed, Blanch, Emil, and Ruby went by train to Carrollton for her funeral. While they were there, Otto decided to start making plans to also move to Colorado. Edna was the reason he had stayed in Missouri; now there was no reason for him not to join the rest of his family.

In 1919, both Creed and Harley finally received their serial patents for their land claims. Their claims now, officially, belonged to them. It didn't take long for Harley and Sis to build a dugout on their claim, and once that was done, Harley built and opened a general store on the northwest corner of Creed and Blanch's claim. There was a growing need for a general store in that area, and building it on Creed and Blanch's claim put it right on the road between Kim and Springfield—a perfect place. Harley and Sis and their three sons, Glen, Wayne, and Ray, lived in the back of the store. They also applied for, and eventually received, approval to open a post office in the store. The establishment date for the post office was February 16, 1920. Harley named the "town" Andrix.

The spring of 1919 once again had good rainfall. In fact, in May, just a month after Jessie was born, it rained for three straight days. Lee and Ethel could do nothing but stay in the dugout and wait for the rain to stop. But on the second day, they noticed that the upper walls of the dugout were becoming wet. Ethel prayed that the rain would stop, and Lee started gathering up things to put in the wagon. It soon became obvious that they could not stay in the dugout any longer, so together, in the pouring rain, they loaded everything they possibly could into the wagon. Around noon on the third day of rain, they hitched up their horse, put covers over Robert and Jessie, and started for Creed and Blanch's claim. As they left, they watched the roof and walls of their home cave in. Their home was gone.

Ethel's sister Nancy had moved to Walker, Colorado, so Creed and Blanch had room for Lee and Ethel to stay with them. Lee immediately, with a lot of family help, began building a new dugout. This time, they built it close to a spring-fed creek that ran through their claim, so water was somewhat more accessible to them than it had been in their first dugout. The new dugout was reinforced with more wood—they even had a wood floor. After digging their stove out of the old dugout, they were able to move into their new home in the ground by the beginning of June.

That year, the world news centered primarily on the ending of World War I. The Treaty of Versailles was signed in the Palace of Versailles near Paris, France, on June 28, 1919. The treaty terms, written primarily to punish Germany, laid full responsibility for the damages caused during WWI on Germany, specifying that Germany owed extremely large sums in reparation to the Allied powers. In addition, major land concessions were forced upon Germany, including the loss of all colonies, and the German army was limited to one hundred thousand men. Germany, with no military power left to resist, had no recourse but to sign the treaty. The nations of the world were reported as being hopeful that WWI would be "the war to end all wars"—the nations of the world, that is, with the exception of Germany.

There was also important national news in June 1919. Newspapers were filled with reports of President Wilson's attempt to get the Nineteenth Amendment to the US Constitution passed and ratified. The Nineteenth Amendment would give women the right to vote in all state and national elections. Finally, by June 1919, the amendment was passed by both the House and the Senate. The ratification process had begun.

AND…the 1919 city directory of Pueblo, Colorado, showed that Frank and Bessie Parise lived there. Frank was a meat cutter. They had been living in Pueblo, about 125 miles northwest of Kim, since their marriage, two years earlier. They were married on September 5, 1917. In 1919, Frank and Bessie Parise were both completely unknown to Lee, Ethel, or anyone else in the Winfrey family. However, that would eventually change.

Lee and Ethel worked hard to salvage everything they could from their original home site. The barn and fences were moved, and soon they had more beans and corn planted. Once they were established in their new home, Lee left again to find work in Trinidad. By now, Ethel was getting used to his trips to Trinidad. She hated for him to be gone, but he always returned with badly needed money and supplies, so she never asked him not to go. And when he was gone, there was no time to feel sorry for herself. There was just too much work to be done, leaving little time to do anything but survive. Good corn crops were essential to feed the horse, cow, chickens, and pigs. Good bean crops were essential to feed themselves. Each time Lee was away, it was up to Ethel to do it all. That also included keeping the JJ cattle out of the corn—which was a daily challenge.

Despite the exhaustingly hard work, Ethel's spirits remained high. She felt that with their new dugout, they were making some progress. But most important, she always relied on her faith in God to see them through the tough times—her faith was what sustained her.

Fortunately, some of the extremely difficult tasks, like the butchering of a hog, were made easier because the family would gather and share the work. Claude's daughter Irene Winfrey Jones best described this in her book, *Irene and Levi, Our Journey Through Life.* She described the butchering of a hog and the making of soap in chapter 5:

> *Butchering a hog was a family affair and my dad's family was a large family. They all came (men, ladies, and kids) for the event, and sometimes it lasted one or two, and sometimes three days.*
>
> *A large deep hole was dug into the ground, big enough for the vat to put over it. In this hole they built a fire and put the vat over it. They fed the fire with wood until the water came to a boil. My dad used a 30 gallon metal barrel with the top cut out and put it in the hole.... When the water came to a boil, the stove ashes or a can of Lewis Lye was added. The lye made the hair come loose from the hide quicker. They scalded one hog at a time, and it took them some time to get it scalded....*
>
> *My dad had built a pulley to handle the hog in the barrel. When the hair began to slip off, it was time to swing the hog onto the platform.*

Then two men would start scraping the hair from the hide. When all the hair was scraped off, the hog was swung with the pulley to the windmill and would be gutted.... Usually it would stay hung on the windmill over night or until the meat would cool out.

Most of the men would do a good job of scraping the hog except for the feet, head and ears, but Dad seemed to forget them. I would have to clean them later, and it was so hard to get all of the hair scraped off. The ears, head, skin and tongue were used to make head cheese and it was very important to clean them thoroughly. When I was growing up there was not waste. Dad even saved the bladder and washed it out and blew it up and made us kids a ball to play with. We never knew what a real ball was. Dad made the head cheese and liver worst. If no one butchered with us, we would always share our meat.

Usually it took Dad and I several days to get the meat all processed, and put away. Then it was time to make soap.

Dad began to trim the fat from the ham, shoulders, and backbone and the fat was put into a large black pot to render up for lard. The lard was put into ten and twenty gallon crock jars and stored in a cool place, and usually ours went into the basement. Then the fat was cut from the intestines and rendered for making soap.

The recipe for making soap was always on the outside of the can of Lewis Lye. There were so many pounds of cracklings or stale lard. It usually took two or three cans of lye to so many quarts of water—cook until the lye ate up all the cracklings and the soap was smooth and then was poured into a container to let cool. Some people put different kinds of perfume into the mixture to make it smell good. When it cooled we would cut it into three or four-inch squares and put it on a flat object to cure. This lye soap made the clothing smell so good and look so clean.

All of these processes took days, and everyone shared in the work. But because of all that hard work and family togetherness, once the 1919 fall trip to the cedars had been made, Lee and Ethel were ready for another winter.

Irene described the men's fall trip to the cedars in chapter 4 of *Irene and Levi, Our Journey Through Life*:

> *Every Fall my dad, Claude, and his dad, Creed, and his 2 sons went to the cedars, south of Higby, Colorado. My Granddad Creed and his family had filed on some land about 35 miles west of Pritchett, Colorado.... My dad would hook 2 wagons together and hitch 4 horses to the front wagon and pull another wagon. He would go to Andrix and all of the men would go together to the cedars. There would be 8 different wagons. It would take Dad 2 days to drive to Andrix and one more day for all of them to get to the cedars. They camped out while chopping the wood and putting it in the wagon. My dad would be gone 2 or 3 weeks. We still lived on the claim west of Two Buttes.*

Higbee, Colorado, was forty miles north of Kim, on Highway 109.

When Lee returned from the 1919 trip to the cedars, he surprised Ethel with the news that he had decided to squeeze in another quick trip to Trinidad. He usually did not travel this close to the cold weather, but he seemed determined to go, and he assured her that he would be home before the start of the bad weather, with money and supplies.

She did so hate to see him go this time. It seemed as though every time he was gone, something bad happened—and this time was no exception. A few days after he left, the weather turned chilly. Ethel built a fire in the stove to warm the dugout. The next morning, she awoke to the sight of a large rattlesnake curled up outside against the warm window. She had no choice: she would have to go out and kill that snake. She grabbed her garden hoe, thinking she would first scare it away from the window, but to her surprise, the snake heard her coming. It was coiled against the glass, ready to strike. Without hesitation, she hit the snake where it was coiled, killing it. But in doing so, she shattered the window. It was a disaster: cold weather was right around the corner, and the long trip to Lamar to get new glass could not be made until Lee returned. She covered the broken window as best she could, and Lee returned home before the start of the extremely cold weather—as promised. They made the trip to Lamar to get glass for the window, just in time for the start of another Colorado winter.

Creed Benjamin Winfrey. Circa 1885.

Mary Alice Brown Winfrey - Creed's first wife. Circa 1885.

Daniel Nugent Lynch. Circa 1906.

Dan Lynch and Mae Winfrey's wedding picture - March of 1906.

Blanch's father, John Smith. Date of picture unknown.

Creed's family in 1899. Back row from left to right: Blanch (Creed's wife), Claude, Mae, Gertie, Otto, and Harley (the children standing are the children of Creed and Mary Alice).
Seated are, left to right. Creed, Nancy and Sue (the twins), and Mary Ethel. The three seated children are the children of Creed and Blanch.

William Claude Winfrey and Otto Orphus Winfrey.
Date of picture unknown.

Creed and Blanch with their five children.
Seated from left to right: Emil, Creed, Blanch, Ruby.
Standing from left to right: Nancy, Ethel, Sue. Circa 1915.

Emil Winfrey at a young age. Date of picture unknown.

Creed's oldest three children from left to right: Gertie, Claude, and Mae.
Date of picture unknown.

Gertrude (Gertie) Grace Winfrey. Date of picture unknown.

Harley Winfrey at a young age. Date of picture unknown.

Nancy Elizbeth Winfrey Simmons (twin of Sue). Nancy died in childbirth in Colorado in 1922. Date of picture unknown.

The California Limited.

The Lamar, Colorado train station in 2017.

Ethel and her children in 1926. Robert is standing. Jessie, Melvel, and Margie are sitting on the running board of "Blackbird". Jessie is holding Dortha.

The Bailey children from left to right: Dortha, Jessie, Robert, Melvel, and Margie. Date on this picture is 1928, which means it was taken in Fairfield, California, when Ethel was working for the Winters Canning Company.

Picture of the Prairie Star school teacher's quarters and horse barn which was one of the CWA projects that Robert helped build in 1933. The school house is gone, but the foundation remains. Picture taken in 2017.

One of the three remaining buildings of Andrix, Colorado. The Andrix store and post office, built by Harley Winfrey, was directly across the dirt road seen to the left of this building. Someone has written "Andrix, gone but not forgotten" on the front of this building.
Picture taken in 2017.

Ethel and Mae in Siloam Springs, Arkansas in 1934.

Emil's truck that was used to move Ethel and her children to Flint, Oklahoma in 1935.

Mary Ethel Winfrey Bailey Whetzel. Picture taken in the 1950s.

Leander (Lee) R. Bailey. Date of picture unknown.

CHAPTER 8

1920: The Model 40 Maytag

THE EARLY PART OF THE YEAR 1920 WAS A SIGNIFICANT TIME IN US history. On January 17, 1920, the Eighteenth Amendment, which had been passed and ratified a year earlier, became law. The amendment, known as the National Prohibition Act, established the legal definition of intoxicating liquors and banned the sale of alcoholic beverages meeting that definition.

In March 1920, Robert turned four years old, and Jessie turned one in April. The spring weather was again a welcome reprieve from the long winter. On May 14, 1920, they received the papers showing that Lee's serial patent for their 320-acre land claim had been issued to him. It was exciting to see the name "Leander R. Bailey" on the Bureau of Land Management Serial Patent Document, and to see the exact land description: the north half of Section 29, Township 31 South, of Range 52 West, of the sixth principal meridian. Suddenly, all the hard work seemed worth it. It was cause for a happy celebration—the land was finally, officially theirs. Lee tacked the land patent document on a board, and they proudly displayed it in the corner of a window.

There was more good news for the Winfrey family that spring. Otto, who was still mourning the death of his wife, had left Missouri and moved to Baca County, Colorado, close to Claude and Erma. With Otto now in Colorado, Gertie was the only one of Creed's ten children who remained in Missouri.

Ethel found comfort in being close to her family. Their presence made Lee's repeated absences easier to bear. Lee and Ethel got their

1920 spring corn and beans planted, and as soon as that was done, Lee left again for Trinidad.

AND...sometime in 1920, Frank and Bessie Parise left Pueblo, Colorado. The 1920 census shows that they were living in Trinidad. Frank was twenty-eight and a car inspector for the railroad. Bessie was twenty-one, with no occupation listed. Also living with Frank and Bessie were Frank's adopted daughter, Lois Parise, age six, and Frank's brother Joe Parise, age twenty-four.

AND...after Frank and Bessie Parise moved to Trinidad, Bessie's and Lee's paths crossed. Nothing is known of how their affair began, but it *is* known that sometime in 1920 in Trinidad, Lee became involved in a relationship with the wife of Frank Parise.

The news of 1920 continued to report exciting changes in the country and around the world. In August 1920, it was reported that the first local radio broadcast had been aired by a station in Detroit, Michigan. Radios were beginning to become available and affordable for many Americans; soon people all over the United States, and the world, would be able to receive instant news and entertainment. The next significant national news of the year was that the longtime battle fought by the women's suffrage movement finally came to an end with the ratification of the Nineteenth Amendment, in August 1920. On November 2, 1920, Warren G. Harding was elected president of the United States, in the first presidential election in which women had the right to vote in all forty-eight states.

That year, Lee returned home from one of his trips to Trinidad with a grand surprise. Loaded in the back of his wagon was a Model 40 Maytag washing machine! He was beaming as he insisted that Ethel hide her eyes while he uncovered it. He had found some work in the Model T sales business in Trinidad, and he had made more money on this trip than ever before. So he decided that since they now had easier access to water, it was time to try out a Maytag. Ethel had read about, and seen pictures of, Maytag washing machines, but she had never dreamed of having one. It was a tub on legs, with a hand-powered agitator in the middle of the tub and a hand-powered wringer attached to the side. A plug in the bottom made for easy draining. They immediately moved the washing machine out beside the creek, filled the tub with water, and began washing clothes. Ethel thought that this was the finest thing Lee had ever done—finally, no more washtubs, no more washboards, no more hand wringing of clothes. She was delighted by and grateful for such a wonderful surprise.

Toward the end of August 1920, Ethel realized that she was once again expecting. She immediately told Lee the news and was a little disappointed that he did not seem as excited as she wanted him to be. But she understood. Their life was anything but easy, and he seemed to be trying hard to make it easier for both of them. She had to face the hard fact that a new baby would not help make things easier.

In the fall of that year, the Winfrey family had another reason to celebrate. Ethel's sister Nancy returned from Walker, Colorado, and met and married Beverly Simmons, the brother of Harley's wife, Sis. The family gathered together to celebrate the marriage on November 10, 1920.

Soon after the wedding, Lee returned to Trinidad. It seemed to Ethel that each time he went there, the "short-term" work he found lasted a little longer. He returned home before the first snow, and they settled in for another long winter.

CHAPTER 9

1921 to 1922: Children's Mercy Hospital

THE YEAR 1921 STARTED OUT WITH NEWS FROM DAN AND MAE. THEY had found 240 acres of good homesteading land, had moved onto the land, and had staked their claim. The land was partially in Huerfano County and partially in Las Animas County, near Aguilar. It was not far from the Cameron Mine—Dan was still working for the Colorado Fuel and Iron Company, still mining coal at the Cameron Mine. However, their claim was closer to the Lester Mine, so Dan was hoping to be moved to the Lester Mine soon. They seemed to be doing well, and that was great news for Ethel. She missed Mae more than she ever let anyone know.

Sometime in February, Lee started making plans to return to Trinidad. He was excited about the growing automobile industry, and about the connections he had made in Trinidad that could possibly help him pursue that interest. In March, even though Ethel was six months pregnant, she knew how anxious he was to return to Trinidad, so she told him to go. They needed any money he could make, and he was eager to take up where he had left off, the previous fall, in the automobile sales business. As soon as the weather began to hint at the arrival of spring, Lee left for Trinidad.

This time, when he left, Ethel had an uneasy feeling, maybe even a feeling of dread. Perhaps it was the pregnancy, or maybe it was the worry that he would probably be gone for an even longer time than usual. Robert's fifth birthday was coming up, and Ethel hated that Lee was, undoubtedly, not going to be home for it.

It helped that Erma and Claude were expecting the birth of their third baby. Soon Ethel, Blanch, and the children were on their way to Claude's claim to help with the new arrival. There were many Winfrey cousins at Claude's claim to help celebrate Robert's birthday that year. Four days later, Erma and Claude had a son, Benjamin P. Winfrey.

After Benjamin was born, Ethel returned home to their claim. On April 14, Jessie turned two years old; Lee had missed another birthday. Ethel was again disappointed, but she told herself repeatedly that he was doing everything he could to make things better for them.

Despite the fact that she was seven months pregnant, it was up to Ethel to do the spring planting. Lee sent word that the car sales business was going well, so he was staying a while longer—just as she had feared. It was that spring that Ethel first began to rely so much on Robert. Even though he was only five, he helped her with everything. She continued to rely on her faith in God for strength, and she realized she was relying more and more on Robert for help and support.

AND…it appears that when Lee returned to Trinidad, a different kind of news was waiting for him there. Based on the information in Bessie and Frank Parise's divorce papers, when Lee got back to Trinidad in the spring of 1921, Bessie, in all likelihood, informed him that she was pregnant with his baby and that she was leaving her husband, Frank. The divorce papers, filed by Frank a year later (on October 6, 1922), show that Bessie "deserted" Frank in April 1921 and went to Kansas. Apparently, Bessie left Trinidad for Kansas, and Lee went back to his family in Andrix—in time to be home for the birth of his third child.

Blanch was staying at Lee and Ethel's claim toward the end of May, so that she would be there for the birth of their next baby. On May 27, 1921, Ethel gave birth to another boy, Melvel Carl Bailey. Once the baby was born, Blanch became unusually quiet. Ethel could hear the baby crying as Blanch washed him off, so she knew he was alive. Blanch wrapped him in a blanket and handed him to Ethel; he had blond hair with a tint of red. But she could tell by the look on Blanch's face that something was wrong. Blanch went out to get Lee as Ethel laid the baby on the bed and unwrapped the blanket.

As Lee walked in, she began to cry. The heel of the baby's left foot was turned on its side and his toes pointed almost completely backward. Lee took one look at the baby's foot and told her that they would make a trip to see Dr. Verity as soon as possible. Within a few days, they were on their way to Dr. Verity's office in Two Buttes.

Dr. Verity did not waste words: he quickly told them that in order for Melvel to ever walk, orthopedic surgery to straighten his foot would be required. He assured them that the problem was correctable, but the surgery would have to be done sometime within the next eighteen months. The thought of this was frightening to Ethel. The places where this kind of surgery could be done were far away, and she knew it would be expensive. Seeing her fear, Lee assured her that he would get the money, and they would do whatever needed to be done.

AND…on August 9 of that same year, two and a half months after Melvel was born, Bessie Parise gave birth to a son in Kansas. She named him William C. Bailey. It appears that "Bailey" was the correct surname for William. Bessie and Frank Parise's divorce papers, completed on December 14, 1922 (sixteen months after William was born), state that there were no children from the marriage. The divorce was filed by Frank and not contested by Bessie.

Just a few days after Melvel was born, it began to rain. It was one of those long, hard rains that lasted several days, and once again Lee and Ethel grew worried about the dugout. This time it withstood the storm, but the small creek that ran through their claim, the one beside which they left the Maytag, flooded severely. Once the rain stopped, they emerged from the dugout, only to discover that the Maytag had been washed away. Ethel was heartbroken. Her most beloved gift from Lee was gone.

Soon after the flood, newspapers reported that severe flash flooding of the Arkansas River and the Fountain Creek had occurred, killing 1,500 people and inflicting over twenty million dollars' worth of damage around Pueblo. After reading about the flooding in and around Pueblo, Lee and Ethel felt relief that all they had lost was the Maytag.

That rainstorm convinced Lee that he was finished with dugout living. With the help of Creed, Claude, Harley, Otto, and Emil, he immediately began building an above-ground rock-and-mortar house. The house was completed soon, and they were able to move out of the dugout. The house had two rooms, a wood floor, and in all likelihood the same type of roof that was used over the dugouts. It was a little closer to the small stream than the dugout, which would continue to be used for cool storage in the summer.

They had barely gotten settled in the new house when Dr. Verity paid them a visit to report some good news. He had written a letter to Children's Mercy Hospital in Kansas City, Missouri, about Lee and Ethel's situation and Melvel's need for surgery. The hospital had been founded in 1897 by Dr. Katharine Berry Richardson and her sister, Dr. Alice Berry. Dr. Richardson was a surgeon, and Dr. Berry was a dentist. The two sisters had founded the hospital as a not-for-profit, to provide free hospital care for poor and ill children, many of whom were orphans.

It had taken a while, but Dr. Richardson had written back to suggest that they plan to do the surgery on Melvel's foot in August of the next year, 1922. Once Ethel and Lee knew that Dr. Richardson would do the surgery, they began making plans. Lee would sell their best cow to get the needed money for Ethel to take all three children, Robert, Jessie, and Melvel, on the train to Kansas City. Melvel would be sixteen months old. Dr. Richardson sent word that there would be a place at the hospital for them to stay, and a caretaker would be provided for Robert and Jessie while Ethel helped care for Melvel after the surgery. Lee sent a letter to his sister Edna, who lived in St. Joseph, Missouri, asking her to go to Kansas City to help in any way she could.

Ethel liked living in the rock house above ground, although she and the kids would often go to the dugout during the hottest times of summer to stay cool. Lee was home off and on throughout that summer. In the fall of 1921, instead of going to Trinidad, he told Ethel that he had heard of a potential opportunity in the automobile business in Salida, Colorado, and he was going there to see about it. Salida was much farther away, but he felt sure that that was where he needed to be.

He was beginning to get interested in buying used cars and doing needed repairs to fix them up for resale.

Ethel spent that fall preparing for the oncoming winter. The move to the rock house presented a new problem. It would be harder to keep the house warm, and much more wood would be needed for the stove.

Lee arrived home from Salida before the cold weather. This time, he had another surprise: he had purchased a used Model T Ford. He had hauled it home with his wagon. He was going to get it fixed up and running—they were moving into the age of the automobile! Ethel was more concerned about keeping the house warm through the coming winter than the car that didn't run, but Lee's enthusiasm was once again contagious, and she admitted that it would be great to have a car. Lee set off for the cedars and brought in an extra supply of wood.

That first winter in the rock house was difficult. In order for the house to stay warm, the second room had to be closed off. Many times, Ethel felt as though they should just move the stove back into the dugout, which was so much easier to heat. But Lee kept the stove burning as hot as possible, and they stayed in the rock house. When they let the fire die down in order to cook, the house would become cold. They mostly existed on cold pork and beans and foods that Blanch would send over whenever possible.

The family Christmas at Blanch and Creed's claim was a welcome relief. That Christmas Ethel's sister Nancy announced to the family that she and her husband, Beverly, were expecting a baby. The family was overjoyed for them. It would be their first. Nancy had filed a land claim prior to her marriage, and she and Beverly were in the process of proving up that claim.

After Christmas, it was back to the cold rock house. That winter was their sixth in Colorado, and it seemed to Ethel to be the longest one yet—she thought the warm weather would never come. But they made it, and by early spring Lee had the Model T shined up and running. Ethel had never seen him so excited. Now he would be able to do his traveling by car.

The following year, 1922, started out the same as always. Lee began preparing to go back to Salida, and Ethel once again knew that she would probably have to do the spring planting herself. In March, Robert turned six; in April, Jessie turned three; and Melvel turned one the following month. Lee came home from Salida in late spring, pulling another used car. He told Ethel that he'd had several opportunities to sell his car for much more than he had paid for it, and he was excited about fixing up another to take back to Salida to sell.

AND…the divorce papers of Frank and Bessie Parise, which contain Frank's sworn statement of desertion, show that sometime after Bessie left Frank in Trinidad, Frank began looking for her. According to the statement, in July 1922, he found her living in Salida, Colorado. On October 6, 1922, Frank filed for divorce on the grounds of "desertion for more than one year last past." The divorce summons was served to Bessie ten days later in Salida.

By mid-summer, Ethel was getting things ready for the trip to Kansas City. Lee's sister in St. Joseph, Missouri, had written back to say that she would probably not be able to go to Kansas City while Ethel and the children were there. Blanch offered to go with her, but Ethel knew that Blanch was needed in Colorado. Nancy's due date was expected to be about the same time as Melvel's surgery. Ethel assured Blanch that she would be fine. Dr. Verity sent a letter to Dr. Richardson to tell her when Ethel and the children would be arriving in Kansas City, and he asked if there could be someone at the train station to meet them. They would board the train in Lamar on Sunday, August 13, and arrive in Kansas City the next day. Melvel's surgery, according to Dr. Richardson, would be performed sometime that week, after all the necessary tests had been run. Everything was arranged.

That August, Claude and Erma decided to sell their house on the prairie and move into the town of Two Buttes, so that Irene, their oldest daughter (at age six), could start school in Two Buttes that fall. Robert would also be starting school in the fall, after they had returned from Kansas City.

However, the week before Ethel and the children were to leave, a Winfrey family tragedy occurred. That week Ethel's sister Nancy went into labor. Blanch and Ethel were there to help, but Nancy had severe childbirth complications, and both she and the baby boy died. Nancy was the twin of Sue. She was twenty-six years old. The family gathered, and Nancy and the baby were buried together in the Andrix cemetery. Her headstone reads, "1896–1922, Nancy E. Simmons and baby son."

The deaths of Nancy and her baby were a shock to the Winfrey family. Ethel had never seen her mother in such a state of sorrow. For the first time, she heard her mother say that she wanted to leave Colorado. They were just too isolated from everything. Blanch was sure that if Nancy had been under the care of a doctor, she would still be alive. That was almost too much for her to bear.

A few days after Nancy's burial, Lee took Ethel, Robert, Jessie, and Melvel to the train station in Lamar. Ethel had hoped that Lee would go to Kansas City with them, but he insisted that he had important work to do in Salida. Ethel boarded the train with Melvel in her arms, Robert tugging Jessie behind her. She had no idea what lay ahead, but she knew that her faith in God would see them through. She relied heavily on that favorite Bible verse: *"I can do all things through Christ which strengtheneth me"* (Philippians 4:13).

When they arrived at the Kansas City train station, a woman by the name of Mrs. Rhodes was there to meet them. Mrs. Rhodes worked at Children's Mercy Hospital, and she had volunteered to help Ethel throughout Melvel's surgery. They were given a room to stay in at the hospital. Mrs. Rhodes stayed with Robert and Jessie while Ethel tended to Melvel. Dr. Richardson did the surgery that week and was able to straighten Melvel's foot to almost the normal position. After the surgery, Melvel was fitted into a brace on his lower leg, which held his foot in place. Dr. Richardson explained that Melvel would have to wear the brace for at least two years, and it would have to be adjusted as he grew. He would have to learn to walk in the brace. Ethel didn't know how that would ever happen, but Dr. Richardson assured her that he would be able to do it.

After two weeks in the hospital, Melvel was released, and Ethel and the children boarded the train back to Colorado. This time, the trip was more difficult, because the brace made Melvel harder to carry. It was heavy and cumbersome, but with Robert's help, they managed.

Lee met them at the train station in Lamar in another "fixed-up" car. He was happy to report that he had sold another car; his automobile refurbishing business was going well. Lee was also happy to tell Ethel that her brother Otto was getting married. Otto was Ethel's half-brother, whose wife, Edna, had died in Missouri three years earlier. After moving to Colorado, Otto had met, and was now marrying, Valeria Randall. Valeria's parents, William and Clara Randall, were homesteading the 320 acres just east of Harley's claim. Ethel knew Valeria and was happy for Otto. Their wedding would be in Two Buttes on August 30.

It was at Otto and Valeria's wedding that everyone learned that Claude and Erma's three children, Irene, Creeda, and Benjamin, were desperately ill. Claude came to the wedding, primarily to alert everyone. He reported that all three children had severely high temperatures, and Dr. Verity was pretty sure it was typhoid fever, a diagnosis that was, in those days, almost certainly a death sentence. Dr. Verity had quarantined their house. Claude asked everyone to pray, and to stay away. Irene described their struggle with typhoid fever in chapter 8 of *Irene and Levi, Our Journey Through Life*:

> *While we lived in Two Buttes, we older kids had typhoid fever. In those days there were no shots to give children and adults so they would not take the fever. Typhoid fever was so contagious. All three kids in bed at the same time, sick with the fever. It was so hard on my mother. People were so afraid of it that my dad could not hire anyone to come and help. There was not much that could be done for the fever. Our good, ole Dr. Verity came day after day to look in on us. It seemed for days and days we never had any food in our stomachs, and the doctor said liquid diet. For weeks our diet consisted of just eggnog. It was made out of raw eggs, milk, sugar and vanilla. My sister almost died when her fever broke. They sponged her off with alcohol to keep her alive. For days our fever was very high. We were unconscious a lot of the time. We were in*

bed 6 weeks. Our stomachs were so raw and that is why we had to be fed eggnog. For a week or more we never had anything to eat.... We were just skeletons when we began to recover. My mother was just wore out from taking care of us 3 kids.

The diagnosis of typhoid fever was eventually confirmed by Dr. Verity, based on the severity of the illness and the length of time of the children's recovery. But thanks to Erma's determination, all three children survived, and finally, the whole family could gather to help Claude and Erma recover from a difficult six weeks.

Otto wasn't the only member of the Winfrey family to marry that year. Emil, Ethel's youngest brother, had become good friends with Lola Winters, one of Ruby's friends from school. Lola's parents, Wiley and Mary Winters, had staked a claim in the Kim area the same year as all the Winfreys, 1916. Emil had met Lola at church. Exactly five days after Otto and Valeria's wedding, Emil and Lola, with Ruby's help, eloped. They went by horseback to catch a train to Clayton, New Mexico, where they were married on Labor Day, September 4, 1922. Emil was twenty-one years old, and Lola was sixteen.

During the early 1920s, the town of Kim experienced significant growth, and by 1922 its population was about two hundred. It was becoming a thriving little prairie town, the hub of the surrounding farming area. The people of the Kim community were optimistic about the future of their town. In 1922, the *Kim-Country Record*, a weekly newspaper, was founded by Victor L. Waters, the postmaster of the Kim post office.

That fall of 1922, Robert started first grade at the Prairie Star School. Ethel's little sister Ruby was in the sixth grade the year that Robert started first grade, and Harley's sons, Joe and Wayne, were in the second and fourth grades. The Kim school district now had four bus routes throughout the area, so Ruby, Joe, Wayne, and Robert all took the school bus to and from the Prairie Star School, boarding it at the Andrix store. By the time Robert started school, Ethel had learned to drive, so getting Robert to the Andrix store was easy when Lee was home with the car.

In the later part of December 1922, Ethel realized that she was going to have a Christmas surprise for Lee that year. She was once again expecting. It appeared that this baby would be due around the first of September.

CHAPTER 10

1923 to 1925: Aguilar, Trinidad, and St. Joseph

THE SECOND WINTER IN THE COLD ROCK HOUSE WAS JUST AS HARD AS the first had been. Lee was exasperated by trying to keep the house warm, and so was Ethel. That winter, Lee told Ethel that he thought they should move to Aguilar. The move would put him much closer to Salida, where he was successfully buying used cars and reselling them, and they would also be close to Dan and Mae. Ethel was torn. It would be wonderful to live closer to Mae, but she would be much farther away from the rest of the family.

Lee left early that spring of 1923, and returned with news that he had found a house in Aguilar and rented it. They could move as soon as Robert was out of school. Along with news of the move to Aguilar, Lee arrived home pulling another car to fix up for resale.

Robert turned seven that March and spent the spring helping his father fix up the used car. There was no crop planting that spring because of the move. Jessie turned four in April, and Melvel turned two in May. Melvel had learned to stand alone in his brace, but walking was going to be more difficult, since he had no movement in his ankle. Dr. Verity assured Ethel that Melvel would eventually learn to walk with the brace, and Robert was determined that he would. Ethel was amazed at Robert's patience. Every day, Robert would hold Melvel up and try once more to help him walk. Eventually Melvel was actually walking, but only with his brother's support.

That May, Ethel followed Lee to her mother and father's claim, cow, chickens, and horse and wagon in tow. They would leave them with

Creed and Blanch. When they told Ethel's parents that they were moving to Aguilar, Ethel was surprised that Blanch was glad to hear of their decision. She was happy that they would be living in a town, and she expressed her hope that Ethel would have a doctor to help with the birth of their next baby. The traumatic deaths of Nancy and Nancy's baby continued to have a deep impact on Blanch. She suffered from severe sorrow, and her desire to leave Andrix grew more intense every day. Blanch told Ethel that she was hoping they could move back to Missouri soon. Ethel was saddened that her mother had given up, but she didn't blame her. The long, harsh winters and the isolation of the prairie were too much. On the way back to the rock house, Ethel told Lee that she was glad they were moving to Aguilar. After talking to her mother, she felt that it must be the right thing for them to do.

The next day, they loaded everything they could into Lee's car and the refurbished car. Ethel and Jessie followed Lee, Robert, and Melvel to Aguilar. The house Lee had rented was only a few miles from Dan and Mae's claim, and Ethel was excited to be close to Mae again. However, her joy and excitement didn't last long. They had no more than unloaded the cars when Lee told her that he was pulling the refurbished car to Trinidad to sell it. Ethel was sad to see him leave, as always, but she was grateful that he was going to Trinidad to do business, instead of Salida. Trinidad was just twenty miles south of Aguilar.

Lee spent a good deal of that summer of 1923 going back and forth between Aguilar and Trinidad, but he was home on September 2, when Ethel went into labor. That day, Ethel gave birth to their fourth child, a girl whom they named Margie Madeline Bailey. Mae and some neighbors were there to help, and the delivery went well—even without a doctor. As soon as Margie was handed to her, Ethel could see that she finally had a baby who looked like her. Margie had brown hair without a hint of red—she was a Winfrey baby—and Ethel breathed a sigh of relief when she saw that Margie's feet were both perfectly straight.

Not long after Margie was born, Lee went back to Trinidad with the intention of finding a place there to rent. He had decided that they should move again, this time to Trinidad. He told Ethel that the refurbished automobile business was looking better in Trinidad than in Salida. It did not take him long to find a place—a two-room upstairs apartment—and soon they were loading up the car again and moving to Trinidad.

Lee told Ethel that she would like Trinidad, the county seat of Las Animas County. The population was about eleven thousand. He told her that Trinidad had everything: modern schools, a library, churches, a theater, grocery stores, furniture stores, and even a Woolworth's. They were now going to be "city folks." Robert was seven years old, Jessie was four, and Melvel was two. Melvel had been in his brace for a year. Ethel was happy to see how excited Robert seemed to be about moving to the city.

Lee's enthusiasm was contagious yet again, and Ethel made up her mind to be happy about the move—especially with winter coming on. The apartment had conveniences she had never had. It had indoor plumbing, radiator heat, and best of all, electricity. For the first time in her life, she could turn a switch and light up the room. Keeping the children warm and clean was going to be so much easier, and the thought of not having to face another winter in the cold rock house was a relief. She hated being so far away from her family, but Trinidad was a beautiful place, made even more beautiful by the Purgatoire River that ran through the center of town. Life there was going to be much different from life on the prairie.

Trinidad was often referred to as the "Gateway to the Rockies" because of its location where the Colorado Rockies meet the Great Plains. To the west, Ethel could see the beautiful Sangre de Cristo Mountain Range, to the north were the Spanish Peaks, and no matter where she was in town, she could always see Fisher's Peak. It was a tall mountain toward the south, capped with a mesa that overlooked the entrance to Raton Pass. Lee told her that after you went through Raton Pass, you would be in New Mexico.

Once they got settled in, Lee resumed his traveling. Ethel was surprised that he still needed to travel so much, but she didn't complain—his used automobile business was making a living for them. Robert started the second grade that September, and Ethel was doing her best to adjust to city life, but she stayed worried all the time. She was used to having help from her family when she needed it, and there was no family, at all, in Trinidad.

AND…the Trinidad City Directory for 1924 shows that Bessie James was living in Trinidad and working as a clerk at the Woolworth's there. It appears that Bessie and her son, William, had moved from Salida to Trinidad, probably sometime in 1923. Apparently at the time of the move, she stopped using her married name of Parise and began using her maiden name, James.

Ethel couldn't help but feel isolated from her family, but that feeling was eased a little by the weekly letters she received from her mother. There was always plenty of family news. Claude and Erma, back in Two Buttes, had another baby that year. She was their fourth child. They named her Fern. Emil and Lola also had a baby, their first, a girl named Margie Marveldean. Now Ethel and Emil both had a Margie; Ethel's was six months older than Emil's.

Robert completed the second grade in Trinidad in May 1924. It was that summer, at the age of eight, that he got his first paying job. He worked for the Trinidad Creamery Company and proudly brought the money he earned home to his mother.

Lee was gone most of the time that summer, and the longer he was gone, the more Ethel missed her family. She especially missed home after she received word from her mother that Harley and Sis had decided to move to California. They were tired of the harsh winters in Andrix, and they had sold the Andrix store to Fred and Icie Cox. They were moving soon to Petaluma, California, with their three boys. Petaluma was thirty-five miles north of San Francisco in the beautiful Sonoma Valley. Ethel wished that she could be home to help them pack and see them off. No matter how hard life in Andrix had been, as far as Ethel was concerned, it was still home.

Then another letter arrived that again made Ethel want to be home. Blanch wrote that Claude and Erma's baby daughter Fern was suffering terribly from whooping cough. Ethel wished she could be there to help.

AND...on July 14, 1924, Judge Joseph Newitt of Chafee County, Colorado, signed the decree that granted Frank S. Parise a divorce from his wife, Bessie. The decree stated that "the defendant, Bessie Bernice Parise, willfully and without cause abandoned and deserted the plaintiff, her husband, for more than one year prior to the bringing of this action and continues to do so."

That fall of 1924, Robert started the third grade in Trinidad. He continued to work at the creamery after school. Ethel thought seriously about going back to the rock house because Lee was always gone, but the thought of making a move like that with four children, and one just a year old, was overwhelming. The only way she could do it would be if one of her brothers, or her father, were to come to Trinidad to get them. She decided it was best to stay—at least for a little while longer.

By that September, Melvel had been in his brace for two years, and he was beginning to take a few steps without Robert's help. Ethel had found a "bone" doctor in Trinidad. The doctor adjusted the brace, but he felt that Melvel should stay in it for at least another year.

Toward the end of September, Ethel's weekly letter from her mother told her more good news. Otto and Valeria had had their first child, a boy named Laverne Otto Winfrey. He was born in Two Buttes.

Finally, when the first snow of winter started to fall, Lee came home. He arrived with gifts for the children. When she saw him, Ethel was glad that she had stayed.

Lee stayed home throughout the winter, and in February Ethel realized that she was once again expecting. With spring right around the corner, she knew that Lee would soon be traveling again. The idea of continuing to live in Trinidad, with Lee gone most of the time and a baby due in September, made her decide that she must move home. She told Lee that she didn't want to have their next baby in Trinidad by herself, without her family around. She said she couldn't, and wouldn't, do it. She had made up her mind: she wanted to go back to Andrix. Lee didn't appear to be the least bit surprised. All he said was that he needed to think about it.

Blanch continued to faithfully send family news each week, and Ethel anxiously awaited the arrival of each letter. That March, she received word from her mother that her father had sold his claim site to Claude and Erma, so that their family could move from Two Buttes to Andrix. Blanch and Creed would be moving into a rented house about a half mile from their claim. Ethel was happy that Claude and Erma would be closer to her parents, but this news made her want to go back to Andrix even more.

That March, of 1925, Robert turned nine years old. It seemed to Ethel that he was more of a father figure to his brother and sisters than their own father was. Ethel was depending on Robert more and more, and she was amazed at what a "man" he was becoming—at the age of nine.

It was late in May, when the weather started to warm, that Lee told Ethel that since he would soon be traveling again, a change had to be made, and he had a plan. He told her that after a lot of thought, he had decided that they should move back to Missouri. Ethel was shocked. She had never imagined that he was thinking that. His idea was that they would move to St. Joseph, where his sisters, Edna and Lola, lived. He told her that he would not be able to move to St. Joseph until later, but he wanted Ethel and the children to go right away, so that they would be settled by the time the baby was due. He would be there before the baby was born. In fact, he said he had just sent a telegram to each of his sisters, asking them to help Ethel find a place to live when she arrived.

The idea of going back to Missouri hadn't crossed Ethel's mind, but it was apparent that Lee's mind was made up. She hated Trinidad, and she did think there was a possibility that her mother and father might be moving back to Missouri soon. She never admitted it to anyone, but there had been many, many days when she had longed for the beautiful greenness of Missouri.

After much thought and many prayers, she agreed with Lee that this might be the best thing to do. It would be easy to get to St. Joseph by train, and she needed to take Melvel back to Children's Mercy Hospital in Kansas City to have his foot checked and his brace removed or adjusted. She began to pack. It took only a few days for the arrangements to be made. Lee's sister Lola sent a return telegram saying that she would be expecting them.

Just three days after Lee told Ethel about the move to St. Joseph, he took her and the children to the train station in Trinidad. He gave Ethel enough money to pay for food and rent for several months, and he told her that he would send her money often. As the good-byes were exchanged, Lee said he would see her in St. Joseph soon—he would be there before the baby was due. As the train pulled out of the station, the children pressed their faces to the window to wave good-bye to their father. But he was already gone. Robert was nine, Jessie six, Melvel four, and Margie almost two. Ethel was six months pregnant.

The train trip to St. Joseph was fun for the children, but Ethel left Trinidad anxious and worried. She wondered if she was doing the right thing. But going back to Andrix was all but impossible, and she just couldn't stay in Trinidad any longer. She liked Lola, and Lola had sent a welcoming telegram, so maybe, once Lee got to St. Joseph, everything would be okay.

She prayed during the entire trip, and by the time they got to St. Joseph, she felt better—her faith was strengthening her. Throughout the trip, she repeatedly thought of another Bible verse she had memorized as a child: *"For God hath not given us the spirit of fear; but of power, and of love, and of a sound mind"* (II Timothy 1:7). This verse calmed her fear. She had a sound mind, she was surrounded by the love of her children, and God was giving her the power to do what she needed to do.

Lola and her husband, James Archer, were at the train station to meet them. Lola told her that she had found a two-room house for them and had already paid the first month's rent. Ethel was surprised to hear this. She thought Lola had learned that she was coming to St. Joseph only three days earlier. Lola told her that Lee had sent the money for the rent several weeks prior. Ethel could hardly believe what she was hearing—apparently Lee had begun making arrangements for the move to St. Joseph weeks before he had ever discussed it with her.

The house Lola had found was small, but it had some furniture, and there were neighbors nearby. The house had radiator heat, indoor plumbing, and electricity, and the neighbors had a telephone. Lola had even bought groceries, to help them get settled quickly. Ethel was extremely thankful for Lola's help.

Lola, knowing that Ethel needed to take Melvel to Kansas City, told her that getting there would be easy because of the St. Joseph-Kansas City Interurban Railway. It was an electric-powered train, much like a trolley, that ran back and forth between St. Joseph and Kansas City multiple times a day. It would take only two hours to get to Kansas City on the Interurban. Lola gave her a pamphlet that included the schedule.

Ethel didn't waste any time getting Melvel to Kansas City. Early one morning, she set off for the Interurban station in downtown St. Joseph, carrying Melvel. Robert stayed at the house to take care of Jessie and Margie. Melvel was heavy, but Ethel was determined. She knew she could do it, and she did. Her train ticket was $1.55, and if she held Melvel on her lap, he could ride for free.

Lola had told her that the Interurban traveled fast, but once they were out of the downtown area of St. Joseph, she was surprised by its speed. The conductor had told the passengers, prior to leaving the station, that they would be traveling at speeds of up to seventy miles per hour off and on throughout the trip. Before she knew it, they were there.

She took a trolley to Children's Mercy Hospital, where Dr. Richardson was happy to see them. After her examination, Dr. Richardson adjusted Melvel's brace and recommended that he remain in it for at least another six months. This meant that Ethel would need to return to Kansas City in December. Dr. Richardson also explained that once Melvel was out of the brace, he would need corrective shoes, which would cost forty dollars. Ethel left Dr. Richardson's office sad that the brace would have to stay on for another six months, and worried about the exorbitant cost of the shoes.

The visit to Dr. Richardson's office had taken longer than Ethel thought it would, but she made it to the Interurban station in time to catch the last train back to St. Joseph that day. It was dark by the time she arrived in St. Joseph. She began walking and carrying Melvel in the direction of their house. She walked and walked, always thinking that she was getting nearer to the house, but never finding it. After what seemed like a very long time looking, she knew that she was lost. She realized she had no choice; she would have to ask someone for help. Thankfully, a kind couple saw her struggling to carry Melvel and asked if they could help. She told them that she was trying to get home, but she could not find her house. In her effort to let them know how grateful she was for their help, she told them how badly she needed to be home, because her other three children had been at home all day, alone. The couple was happy to help, and soon, Ethel and Melvel were home.

After her trip to Kansas City, Ethel wrote a long letter to Lee to tell him that Melvel's foot was doing well, but Dr. Richardson had recommended that he stay in the brace at least another six months. She told him that they would need to take Melvel back to Kansas City in December, and she told him about the cost of the corrective shoes. She also wrote that if he wasn't coming to St. Joseph soon, she needed him to send money.

Lee's return letter included some money, which he specifically said was for Melvel's corrective shoes. Those words were a jolt—she wouldn't need the money for the shoes until December. Lee had promised that he would be in St. Joseph by September.

September arrived, but Lee did not—just as she had feared. It was time for Robert to start his fourth-grade year and Jessie to start the first grade, but Ethel knew that school was not going to be possible for them, at least not for a while. She was nine months pregnant, and she had no means of getting them to and from school. She couldn't even spare the money for a decent shirt for Robert to wear. She told Robert and Jessie—and herself—that they would start school just as soon as their father got to St. Joseph, but they may have to start a little late.

On Saturday, September 19, Ethel went into labor. She sent Robert to their neighbor's house to ask them to call a doctor. She also told Robert to call Lola. Lola said she would be there soon. The neighbor's doctor came quickly, but then left and never came back. Lola called a midwife, who arrived in time to help deliver the baby, a beautiful girl with light blonde hair. Ethel named her Dortha Mae Bailey; she was born on September 19, 1925.

When Ethel held her new baby for the first time, a fear came over her that she had not let herself face until then. She made herself accept the probability that this time, with this baby, she may be on her own. She had no idea how she was going to take care of another child, but she loved that baby immediately, and she knew that somehow, she would do it.

The next month, things became even more difficult. Before Dortha was born, Ethel had been visited by people from the Welfare Department of St. Joseph. They told her that someone had reported her to them, and they had come to check on the welfare of the children. They would not tell her who had made the report, but Ethel suspected that it was the couple who had helped her find her house the night she came back from Kansas City with Melvel. On that first visit, Ethel had assured the welfare people that she was doing fine, that she had relatives in St. Joseph who were helping her, and that her husband would be arriving soon.

A few days after Dortha was born, Ethel wrote to Lee to tell him about their new baby, and this time, she told him that she absolutely had to know when he would be coming to St. Joseph. It was in his return letter that he told her the news she had feared: he was not coming to St. Joseph after all.

Soon after she received that alarming letter, the welfare people returned to do another check. This time, they wanted to know everything about everything, and they especially wanted to know why Robert was not in school. Again, she assured them that her family was fine, and that she was enrolling Robert in school soon. But she now had a newborn baby, and this time she had to tell them that her husband would not be coming to St. Joseph. When the welfare people left, she knew they would be back—probably very soon.

The next day, Ethel and Robert, with the four little ones in tow, went to the nearest school, where Robert was enrolled. The school was quite a distance from their house, but with an early start, he could walk. Lola had given her a couple of old shirts, which she quickly sized down to fit him. Robert now had two shirts to wear to school. He was ready to go.

Ever since she had arrived in St. Joseph, her mother had faithfully sent her weekly letters, and there had been many hints that Creed and Blanch were going to leave Colorado soon. Blanch's letters always mentioned how hot and dry things were in Colorado, and always told of the difficulty they were having growing adequate crops. There had been a severe drought on the prairie for the past year. Ethel's return letters to her mother continuously suggested that they come to St. Joseph.

In October, along with all the other bad news, Ethel received a letter from her mother telling her that they were finally leaving Colorado—but not for Missouri. They were loading up their wagon to move to Berryville, Arkansas. Ethel was disappointed, but not surprised, that they were not coming to St. Joseph. Her father was always reading and talking about various parts of Arkansas, so their decision was somewhat expected. Blanch said that she, Creed, and Ruby (now fifteen) would probably be in Berryville by the end of October.

The family news in November of that year was actually worse than in October. In early November, Ethel received a letter from her mother saying that they were getting settled in Berryville. However, the next letter from her mother brought news of another family death. Claude and Erma's third daughter, Fern, the one who had been sick with whooping cough, had died of pneumonia. She was two years old, the same age as Margie. Irene Winfrey Jones described the death of her sister in chapter 8 of *Irene and Levi, Our Journey Through Life*:

> *I was in the 2nd Grade when we lost my little sister, Fern. She was born after we moved into town. Back in those days when a person had pneumonia, it was about certain death. Most of the children and adults did not survive the disease. She had the whooping cough, in fact all 4 of us had it at the same time. My dad also had whooping cough when we had it. I can remember him cranking those Model T Ford trucks. They*

> *were so hard to start. He would crank awhile and sit on the ground and cough a while.... I remember my mother grieving about her.*

Ethel could hardly bear not being with her family during those terrible times. They needed her, and she needed them. But it was just not possible.

For some reason, she continued to cling to a small hope that Lee would eventually come to St. Joseph. He did not, but in December, he sent her money for Christmas presents for the children. That money went toward groceries instead.

CHAPTER 11

1926 to 1927: Back to Andrix

SOMEHOW, ETHEL MANAGED TO STAY IN ST. JOSEPH UNTIL AFTER THE start of the new year, 1926. She needed to take Melvel back to Children's Mercy Hospital in Kansas City, to see if his brace could be taken off. But she couldn't. There was no money for tickets on the Interurban for all of them, and she didn't dare leave the little ones with Robert. The welfare people might pay a visit while she was gone.

Robert was still attending school as often as possible, but they were scarcely making ends meet, and doing so only because Lee sent money—occasionally. Each day was becoming more difficult than the last. She was barely feeding her children, and the welfare people were putting pressure on her. In March, they paid another visit, and this time they gave her a written warning. If she couldn't feed her children, they would take them away from her.

With that warning, she knew they had to get out of St. Joseph, and soon. She had absolutely no other option; she would have to return to the rock house at Andrix.

Immediately after receiving the written welfare warning, she went to a neighbor's house and called Lola, to ask her for the money to get the children back to Colorado. Thankfully, Lola was able to give it to her. She then sent letters to her brothers Claude, Otto, and Emil, telling them that she was returning to Andrix and asking that one of them come to Lamar to get her and the children. The day after the welfare people gave her the warning, she made the trip to Kansas City with Melvel, to get his brace removed and to get his corrective shoes. Feeling confident that the welfare people would not return for a few days, she left Jessie, Margie, and Dortha with Robert.

Later, Ethel would say that seeing Dr. Richardson that day in Kansas City was like seeing an angel. Dr. Richardson understood her situation and offered to help her get back to Andrix. She removed Melvel's brace and fitted him into the corrective shoes. Ethel told Dr. Richardson that she didn't have the money for the shoes, but Dr. Richardson told her that there would be no charge. Ethel left Dr. Richardson's office promising to one day send her the forty dollars.

Within five days of the welfare warning, Ethel had the children on the train, heading back to Andrix. Robert was ten, Jessie almost seven, Melvel almost five, Margie two. Dortha was six months old.

She spent the entire trip back to Colorado praying that her brothers had received her letters, and praying that one of them would be able to come to Lamar. It was hard to imagine going back to the rock house, but it was the only place she had to go. To the best of her knowledge, the house had been empty for three years, so she knew it would take a lot of work to make it livable again. Even though her mother, father, Harley, and Sis were no longer living in Andrix, she still had family there. That thought helped ease her apprehension.

When they arrived in Lamar and stepped off the train, much to her relief, Emil, with his big smile and welcoming hugs, was there waiting for them. Once again, she made the trip from the Lamar train station to the Kim area, only this time, she had five children instead of one, and this time, the trip was in Emil's truck instead of Harley's wagon. It had been exactly ten years since she and Robert had made that same trip with Harley.

On the way, Emil told Ethel about how things had changed in Andrix and around the Kim area since she had left. He was especially happy to report that a Quaker church had been built just west of the Andrix store, on Bill and Sue's claim. Finally, they all had a place in Andrix to attend church on Sundays. He also told her how much the town of Kim had grown. By 1926, the population was almost 500—a twofold increase since she had left. But the lack of rain was the most important change in the area, and Emil was most concerned about that. It looked like their mother and father had decided to go to Arkansas at exactly the right time.

Emil was also excited about the letters they had been receiving from Harley and Sis in California. They loved Petaluma and were doing well there. Every letter was full of good news and descriptions of the beautiful country and excellent weather. They just couldn't say enough good things about California.

The rock house was just as she had expected: empty of everything except the cook stove, but full of dirt. She stayed with Claude and Erma until she could get the house somewhat livable again. It took a lot of work, but her family helped by giving her some beds for the children and a few other pieces of furniture.

The day they moved back in, she and Robert began preparing a garden. She was increasingly amazed at how much she depended on Robert, and what a source of help and comfort he was to her. She and Robert planted corn and beans that spring, but the lack of rain was making it increasingly difficult to grow anything. Robert also helped care for and keep the other children busy. He, Jessie, and Melvel would spend hours roaming the nearby prairie with burlap sacks, picking up dried piles of cow manure, and dragging them home. The prairie provided an excellent supply of cow patties, which were used to start fires in the cook stove.

The dugout where Melvel was born was still there, and after they killed a few rattlesnakes, they were able to use it, once again, for cool storage. Ethel's brothers gave her some chickens and a cow. She was on her way to being able to feed her children.

The entire time they were working on getting resettled in the rock house, Ethel was wondering about Lee. She hadn't written to tell him that she was back in Andrix, and she wasn't sure when she would. However, she didn't have to wonder long. On one of her visits to Claude's homestead, a friend of Claude's told her that he had seen Lee in Trinidad—with another woman. Despite the fact that she had not seen Lee in almost a year, Ethel was surprised at the accusation and unwilling to believe it. The person who claimed to have seen Lee told her that he knew where Lee was working. He was willing to take her to Trinidad so she could see the situation for herself. She accepted the offer. She had no choice; she would have to go to Trinidad to find out the truth.

The trip was miserable. She spent the entire journey trying to prepare herself for the worst—just in case it was true. According to Claude's friend, Lee was working at an automobile dealership, and that was exactly where she found him. Their meeting was cold and short, and when she confronted him about the "other woman," he finally told her the truth about Bessie. And to her astonishment, he admitted that he'd had a child with Bessie.

In an effort to settle things with Ethel, Lee told her that if she would take the child, he would come home to Andrix. Of course, Lee knew she would never do that, and he also knew that he would never return to Andrix. It took a minute for Ethel to compose herself after hearing this absurd suggestion, but once she did, she said exactly what he had set her up to say: under no circumstances would she ever take another child to raise. Lee's compromise and effort to free himself from guilt was to give her some money and a Model T Ford—which she took without hesitation. Within minutes, she left, hoping she would never have to see him again.

That night, she rented a room at a tourist court outside of Trinidad. Feeling completely exhausted, she lay down and cried herself to sleep.

Her drive back to Andrix the next day was, unfortunately, one she would never be able to forget. It took a day to make the drive, so she had a lot of time to do a lot of thinking. Suddenly, all those trips Lee always had to make made sense to her. She was shocked that she hadn't figured things out earlier—or maybe she just never wanted to admit what she had really always suspected. The part that was almost impossible to accept was the astounding revelation that Lee had a child with another woman, a child the same age as Melvel.

Once again, she relied on her faith to help her accept what she had to accept, and to help her have the strength to do what she needed to do. The Bible verse that had helped her get through the grief of Inez's death was the one she relied on now: *"God is our refuge and strength, a very present help in trouble"* (Psalms 46:1). She repeated it to herself over and over during the long drive back to Andrix.

By the time she got back, she had thought everything through, and she had a new determination. Her mind was focused on what she would have to do, and she was ready to do it. Her life with Lee was over, and she was determined, now more than ever, to prove to herself and her children that they could make it without him.

Claude, Otto, and Emil were all waiting for her when she returned. They were there to let her know that she could count on them to help her with whatever she needed. When she told them the whole story, all three were ready to go to Trinidad to pay Lee a visit. Otto didn't mince words; he had known Lee the longest and had never liked him. He told her he was glad that she was rid of him. All three brothers promised to keep track of Lee and pay him "collection visits" whenever they could find him.

She was so very grateful to be back home with her family—she was now absolutely sure that she was right where she needed to be. But the most difficult thing she had to do was tell the children that their father was not coming home. This had little effect on Margie, who was three—she had few memories of him. And Dortha was only nineteen months old. The hard part was telling Robert, Jessie, and Melvel, who were eleven, eight, and about to turn six respectively. Robert took the news like the little man he had become. He hugged his mother and assured her that they were going to be just fine. Jessie spit in the dirt and said she didn't care. Melvel was confused; he said he was sure his father would be back.

That night, Ethel sat down and wrote a long letter to her mother and father—the hardest letter she had ever had to write. She told them she was back in Andrix, and she told them about her trip to Trinidad. She wrote about the "other woman," but she didn't tell them about the "other child." She would wait and tell them that part of the story later—much, much later.

Robert and Jessie started the fourth and first grades at the Prairie Star School that September. Now that Ethel had a car, it was easy to get them to and from school. Ethel decided that they would name the car Blackbird. It suited the situation perfectly: it represented a dark time in her life, and the cause of that darkness had flown away. The children loved the name, which they always used to refer to the car.

A highlight of each day for them all was driving Blackbird to the Andrix post office. It was especially fun when the Sears, Roebuck and Company mail order catalog arrived. The children loved looking through the catalog—it was a light into the world outside the Colorado prairie. They passed it around for days, cutting out pictures they wanted to keep. Once the catalog was no longer new and exciting, it went out to the outhouse, to be used as toilet paper.

In November of that year, the Winfrey family suffered another death. Otto and Valeria had had their second son, William Ralph, on October 11, but he lived for only a month and a half. He died on November 24, 1926, for unknown reasons. The family gathered and mourned together. Ralph was buried in the Kim cemetery.

That fall, newspapers across the country ran interesting and exciting stories about a US highway that was under construction. The highway would eventually run from Chicago, Illinois, to Los Angeles, California—almost 2,300 miles. The newspaper stories gave an outline of the cities and towns that the road would connect and reported that plans were underway to eventually pave the entire highway. Horse-drawn wagons and carriages were rapidly being replaced by automobiles, and wagon trails all over the United States were being smoothed out into roads suitable for cars. The automobile was changing America. The highway between Chicago and Los Angeles was one of the largest road-building undertakings yet. It would be called Route 66.

The oncoming winter was worrisome, as usual. Ethel knew how hard it was going to be to keep the rock house warm, but Robert went with Claude to the cedars, and they brought back a good supply of wood. By the start of the cold weather, she felt that they were as ready as they could possibly be.

Just before that Christmas of 1926, Ethel and the kids drove to the Andrix post office. In addition to her mother's weekly letter, a box had arrived, addressed to her. It had a return address name of Lee Bailey. A note inside simply said, "Christmas presents for the children." Her first instinct was to throw the box in the trash, but it was too late—the children had seen it, and they wanted to know what it contained.

Knowing how much it would mean to them, she let the children open their presents from Lee on Christmas Eve. The gifts were just trinket types of toys, but they made the children happier than she had seen them in a long time. She watched the children's excitement as they opened their presents, and grew madder with each gift. How dare he be the hero, doing something for them that he knew she could not do? That Christmas was a happy and memorable one for the children, but a very sad one for Ethel.

By the start of the new year, Ethel and the children were doing okay. Ethel had become closely associated with the people who attended the Quaker church, and each Sunday, when weather permitted, not only would she and the children attend church, but they would also participate in an after-church potluck dinner. The people of the church were helpful and supportive, and they would send the leftover food home with her. Her prayers each night would always include her thankfulness for those Christian friends.

In March, Robert turned eleven, and he finished the fourth grade that spring. Jessie turned eight in April and finished the first grade. Melvel was doing well in his corrective shoes, but he was growing fast, and Ethel knew that he would soon outgrow them, probably before she ever got them paid for. Her debt to Dr. Richardson for the shoes was constantly on her mind. Her primary thought throughout the rest of that winter was that she needed to get someplace where she could earn some money.

That May, the world news was exciting. The *Kim-Country Record* reported that on May 21, just six days before Melvel turned six, Charles Lindbergh, an obscure US airmail pilot, completed a flight from Long Island, New York, to Paris, France. It was the first solo flight across the Atlantic Ocean and the first nonstop flight between North

America and the mainland of Europe. The world was becoming a smaller place.

But Ethel was more excited about a classified ad she saw in the *Kim-Country Record* that spring for green-bean pickers in Manzanola, Colorado. The ad said that the picking might begin as early as mid-June, and many pickers were needed. Manzanola was about eighty miles northwest of Andrix, just on the other side of La Junta. Finally, she saw an opportunity to make some money.

As soon as Robert and Jessie were out of school, they gathered up everything that would fit in Blackbird and moved to Manzanola. Claude came to the rock house and took her cow and chickens to his homestead.

It was easy to find a place to live in Manzanola. There was plenty of cheap housing for the green-bean pickers. She found a room in town at what she called a boarding house. By the time she and the children arrived, the picking had begun, and she went right to work. She parked Blackbird on the edge of the field, and all five children stayed in and around the car while she picked green beans. She was hoping that Robert could also pick beans, but the field overseer would not allow it—he was too young. However, at the boarding house, one couple was happy to pay Robert to stay with their children while they picked beans. So Robert stayed in town to babysit, while Ethel and the other four children spent the summer in the green-bean field.

That summer of 1927, on July 29, while Ethel and the kids were in the green-bean fields of Manzanola, a man by the name of Frank H. Hall filed a suit against multiple defendants in the Las Animas County District Court. Completely unbeknownst to Ethel, Leander R. Bailey was listed as one of the defendants. The Las Animas County District Court documents for Case #11866 show that Frank H. Hall claimed that he "at the time of the beginning of this suit and for a long time prior thereto was in exclusive possession of said real estate described as the subject matter of this action, and each and every part and portion thereof, and has been in such possession at all times since the beginning of this suit." The real estate in question included the "North half of Section Twenty-nine (29), Township Thirty-one (31) South of Range

Fifty-two (52) West of the Sixth Principal Meridian," which was the legal description of Lee and Ethel's homesteaded claim. The court documents outline the efforts made to contact and summons all defendants, and they specifically state that despite a "diligent search," Leander R. Bailey could not be found.

After that "diligent search," the documents show that the summons was published "in the Chronicle News, a weekly newspaper of general circulation in the County of Las Animas in the State of Colorado, published in Trinidad, Colorado, for a period of five consecutive insertions; That the first publication of said summons was in the issue of said paper bearing day of August 2, 1927, and that the last publication of said summons was in the issue bearing date August 30, 1927." Ethel, having no access to the *Chronicle News of Trinidad*, was completely unaware that Frank H. Hall was in the process of taking title to her land.

When the green-bean picking was done, Ethel and the children returned to the rock house at Andrix, where Robert started the fifth grade, Jessie started second, and Melvel started first at the Prairie Star School. She and Robert had made enough money in Manzanola to buy supplies for the oncoming winter, and to send a little bit of money to Dr. Richardson for Melvel's corrective shoes. The bill was finally beginning to be paid.

That fall, Robert again went to the cedars with Claude, and with the help of her brothers, Ethel prepared for another long winter. The past prairie summer had been hard for everyone in Andrix. It had been another spring and summer of little rain, and it was becoming more and more difficult to bring in good crops. It seemed as though the drier it got, the harder the wind blew. There were days when just getting out in the prairie wind was fearsome. The homesteaders would have to completely cover up to protect themselves from the sandy soil that the wind would sometimes blow with stinging force.

Toward the end of that fall, with a lean winter ahead of them, the Winfrey families began talking about the California that Harley and Sis described in all their letters. Their letters depicted warm summer days and cool summer nights, with daily summer temperatures ranging from eighty to fifty degrees. They described winters as cool and rainy, with seldom ever a frost and average daily temperatures around fifty degrees. The letters made Petaluma sound like heaven, and soon it was decided: the Winfrey families in Andrix would go to Petaluma together, and they would go in January.

As soon as that decision was made, Claude sent a letter to Creed and Blanch in Berryville, telling them that they were all California bound. The travelers would be Claude and his family, Otto and his family, and Ethel and her family. Emil and Lola would be staying in Andrix. Creed's return letter surprised them all. Creed wrote that he, Blanch, and Ruby would be in Andrix in January. They too would be making the trek to California.

That December, of 1927, Ethel realized that the children were talking amongst themselves about the Christmas presents they were expecting from their father. When she heard them talking, she warned them not to expect presents this year, but it did no good. They were all sure that presents would come. As Christmas neared, they asked every day to go to the post office. Ethel realized that this Christmas might be a heartbreaker for the children, but she allowed even herself to be somewhat hopeful. There had been no word from Lee since the previous Christmas, and she had been dealing with the feelings of desertion for the past year. But maybe, just maybe, he wouldn't completely desert his children.

But each trip to the post office was another disappointment for the children, and for Ethel. The expected presents never arrived. When Christmas had passed, the children collectively accepted that their father had forgotten them. Robert was prepared for the disappointment, but Jessie, with her usual air of defiance, let them all know just how she felt about their father—and she told them that they should all feel the same. Ethel was more mad than sad. Thanks to Lee, she had just one more thing to have to deal with.

AND…the 1927 Albuquerque, New Mexico, City Directory showed that Lee and Bessie were living in Albuquerque. He listed his occupation as salesman. Now Bessie was going by the name Bessie Bailey.

CHAPTER 12

1928 to 1929: California Fever

BY JANUARY 1928, CLAUDE AND OTTO HAD SOLD OFF ALL THEIR livestock, and with the money, they had both purchased new Model A Fords. Ethel's Model T was still in good condition, so she was planning to drive it to California. When Creed, Blanch, and Ruby arrived, they all began loading their cars to the brim with blankets, pallets, clothes, and food. Claude and Erma were also loading a trailer, which they planned to pull to California. It would take three weeks to get to Petaluma, and the driving would be rough. The roads were slowly being improved, but they were still old rutted wagon roads through the mountains. They all knew it would be a slow, cold trip. But they had been preparing for it for almost three months, and there was no stopping them now.

Claude, Erma, Irene, Creeda, and Benjamin would be traveling in one car. Irene was eleven, Creeda nine, and Benjamin six. Erma was five months pregnant. Otto and Valeria would be traveling in their car with their three-year-old son Laverne. Valeria was four months pregnant. Ethel would be traveling in her car with Robert (eleven), Jessie (eight), Melvel (six), Margie (four), and Dortha (two). Ruby, who was eighteen, would be doing the driving in Creed and Blanch's car. Blanch was fifty years old, and Creed was seventy-two.

Irene described their journey in chapter 9 of *Irene and Levi, Our Journey Through Life*:

> *In 1928 the Winfrey family got the California Fever. Earlier one of my uncles had moved out there and he said it was grand living in California.*

There were five families left, so we all had a farm sale and left for California in January 1928.

From the proceeds of the farm sale each family bought a brand new Model A Ford car. Those little cars were really loaded down and some were even pulling trailers. We arrived in Trinidad, Colorado the first night. It took us all day to drive to Trinidad. (72 miles) and the second night we stayed the night at Wagon Mound, New Mexico (60 miles). I can remember it was so cold the water pipes were frozen up in the cabin we stayed in. By then Dad had decided he could not pull a trailer fifteen hundred miles over "washboard" and mountain roads. Our trip had just begun so he sold the trailer. My folks had butchered a hog and my mother had canned a lot of food and Dad was the one who was pulling the trailer. The trailer was full of food, clothing and etc. He decided to sell the trailer and he gave all of the food away.

I guess the folks thought they were going to starve to death when we arrived in California.

It took us 3 weeks to drive over "washboard" roads to our destination in California. Petaluma was a beautiful town, so pretty and green. We were used to the prairie grass of Colorado. My mother really loved California.

After a night in Wagon Mound, the Winfrey "caravan" made its way to Santa Fe, New Mexico, where they began the rest of their journey to California on Route 66. Route 66 took them south from Santa Fe to Albuquerque, New Mexico. At Albuquerque, the road turned west toward Flagstaff, Arizona, and the most intimidating part of their trip: the Sitgreaves Pass, between Kingman, Arizona, and the mining town of Oatman. It was a notoriously narrow road, with steep grades and sharp hairpin curves. The Winfreys had read that the best way to get through the legendary pass safely was to not drive it themselves. Local people from Oatman had found that they could make a living helping others maneuver through the pass; they would drive the travelers' cars in reverse through it, so that the fuel would reach the carburetor on the particularly steep sections. The Winfreys had planned in advance to hire these drivers to get them through.

When the Winfreys finally arrived in Petaluma, they found it to be just as Harley and Sis had described: green and beautiful. Their reunion with Harley and his family was full of Winfrey love and enthusiasm. It had been four years since Harley and Sis had moved to Petaluma, and their boys, Glen, Wayne, and Beverly, were now fifteen, thirteen, and eight. With Harley's help, the newcomers found houses to rent, and the men quickly found jobs. Fruit orchards, the poultry industry, and dairy farming were the primary commercial interests in Petaluma in the late 1920s, and all these industries were thriving when the Winfreys arrived in early February 1928. Soon, they were building chicken coops and buying chickens—lots and lots of chickens. Ethel and her children stayed with Harley and Sis in the beginning. Harley had room for more chickens in his henhouse, so Ethel bought a hundred pullets with what little money she had.

Everyone was extremely happy to be in California. They were looking forward to the mild summer weather and the soon-to-be new additions to Claude's and Otto's families.

Ethel began looking for work right away. It was easy for the men to find jobs in Petaluma, but jobs for women were hard to find. After a long search, she finally accepted that her only option was to go to Fairfield, California, about sixty miles east of Petaluma. The Petaluma newspaper reported that jobs were available for both men and women at the Winters Canning Company in Fairfield. The company was one of Fairfield's largest, employing six to seven hundred people for eight months of each year. Ruby was also trying to find a job, and she decided to go to Fairfield with Ethel, to work in the cannery too. When Blanch was told that Ethel and Ruby were going to Fairfield, she knew that she was needed in Fairfield more than she was needed in Petaluma, so she also began packing for the move.

Ethel and her children left for Fairfield first. She had found a rental house listing in the newspaper and had rented it by mail. She loaded everything she had into Blackbird, which mostly consisted of pallets for beds, some pots and pans, a few clothes, and her children. But she was not about to leave those chickens behind. They were her security, and the only guarantee that her children would have something to eat. So she filled Blackbird with beds, clothes, kids, and thirty chickens, and off they went to Fairfield.

It took an entire day to get there, and upon entering town, a policeman pulled her over. As he walked up to her car, Ethel lowered the window just enough to talk through a small opening. She didn't dare lower the window completely—some of her chickens might escape. The officer explained through the narrow opening that he had stopped her because she had no license on her car. It appears that after seeing a car full of kids covered in chicken feathers, he felt sorry for her and simply told her to try to get her car licensed soon. He also gave her directions to the house she had rented.

The house was old and empty, but it had a chicken coop. With the chickens in the coop and the pallets on the floor, they were moved in. Ethel would go to the cannery the next day and hopefully begin to work. Robert would take care of the other four children while she worked, until Blanch arrived. Then if all worked out as planned, Robert, Jessie, and Melvel would finish out the school term in Fairfield, and Blanch would watch after Margie and Dortha while Ethel and Ruby worked at the cannery. Back in Petaluma, Creed moved in with Harley and Sis, and Ruby and Blanch left for Fairfield.

In April, Claude accepted a job offer to work on a chicken farm near Petaluma, and he and his family moved onto that farm. They were living there when Erma went into labor. On May 5, 1928, complete disaster struck—again. Erma was carrying twin boys and died giving birth to them. The twins were born alive. A doctor came and determined that Erma had died of renal poisoning.

The death of Erma devastated Claude. For days, he was in shock—to the point that he had no interest in giving names to his new sons. Irene and Creeda decided on their names; they named them after their father, Raymond Claude and Roy William. Irene described her mother's death in chapter 9 of *Irene and Levi, Our Journey Through Life*:

> *My father landed a job soon after we arrived in Petaluma. Later on we moved out on a chicken ranch and that is where my mother passed away giving birth to the twins on May 5, 1928. Her brother, Ed Borum and*

> *her sister, Ester Rhodes came to California for her funeral. They went back to Oklahoma with her body to Rosston, Oklahoma on a train. I was not old enough to realize what was in store for me, my sister and my brothers. My dad had a rough time dealing with her death and taking care of us. He did the best he could, having food on the table because we always had plenty to eat, but not having enough clothes to wear.*
>
> *We milked cows and raised chickens and farmed corn and beans…. It was hard to keep us in clothes because we grew out of our clothes that were worn out so quickly. Our aunts and neighbors helped us as much as they could but they had their own families to care for. A lot of times we did look like orphans.*

Claude's recovery from the shock of Erma's death was undoubtedly a slow and difficult process, but perhaps he found a bit of hope if he realized that history was repeating itself. He was the father of five motherless children, all under the age of twelve—just as his own father, Creed, had been thirty-seven years earlier. And unbeknownst to Irene, she was in the same situation that Mae had been in, all those years ago. Irene's childhood, at the age of eleven, was suddenly and completely over.

After the twins' birth, Roy was healthy, but Raymond was not. The doctor's diagnosis was that Raymond had been affected by the renal poisoning that had caused Erma's death, and little could be done. Raymond was struggling.

Six weeks after the twins were born, Otto's wife, Valeria, gave birth to their second baby, another boy, whom they named Murrel Benjamin Winfrey. Valeria not only nursed her own baby, but she also nursed Raymond. Because of Valeria, Raymond survived.

The death of Erma not only devastated Claude, it was also an enormous blow to all members of the Winfrey families. Suddenly, California was not such a happy place. Claude stayed on the chicken ranch for a while, but taking care of five children by himself was very difficult, and in October he decided to go back to Andrix. He felt that Andrix was the best place for the children; Irene, Creeda, and Benjamin needed to be in school, and he was having a hard time getting them to school in California. He had friends who could help in Andrix. Andrix was home—and he needed to be home.

Blanch and Ruby sent word that they planned to stay in Fairfield until the end of the canning season, so Creed decided that he would return to Andrix with Claude. He would move back into the house that he and Blanch had left when they had moved to Berryville, which was now owned by Claude. Otto and Valeria decided that they would also go back to Andrix.

By the end of October 1928, Claude and his five children, Creed, and Otto and his family had resettled back in Andrix. Claude found friends who were willing to help take care of his five-month-old twins, and Irene, Creeda, and Benjamin started going back to school. Now they attended a school located just a half mile from their home. It was built on the hill east of Andrix, where the Andrix cemetery is today. It is unknown when this school was first built and first used.

Irene described their return to Andrix in chapter 9 of *Irene and Levi, Our Journey Through Life*:

> *It took us several weeks to drive back to Colorado and this time there were only four families that came back with us.... There were several people that wanted to adopt us kids. I was old enough to know that I didn't want us kids to be separated. Then people wanted to adopt the twins. I really thought Creeda and I could take care of them. So that was when it became known that Raymond was Creeda's baby and Roy was my baby. After we came back to Colorado, and the twins were older, Creeda took care of her baby and I took care of my baby. She and I really loved the twins. We helped all we could. My aunts and uncles had their own families, but two of my aunts volunteered to take one baby apiece to care for.*
>
> *Then we three older kids went to our Grandfather Creed's and stayed with him while Dad got a job working at picking fruit. Living with Granddad is where I learned to keep house and take care of sister, brothers and Granddad. He helped with the cooking and I did the washing and keeping house. Grandmother Blanche moved to Fairfield, California to be with my two aunts.*

Blanch, Ruby, and Ethel managed pretty well in Fairfield that winter. Ruby and Ethel worked eight-hour shifts at the cannery, each making seven and a half cents an hour, for a total of sixty cents a day. If they worked seven days a week, which they often did, they could earn up to $4.20 a week.

It was while Ethel was in Fairfield that, on November 12, 1928, Frank H. Hall's suit was heard in court. The Las Animas County District Court documents for Case #11866 (*Frank H. Hall v. Leander R. Bailey*) show that Leander R. Bailey "failed to appear or to answer or to otherwise plead or move in said action, and was 'for a long time in default after service of summons' and that 'default and judgement has been regularly entered against' " him. The suit was heard by Judge A. F. Hollenbeck, who ordered "that the plaintiff (Frank H. Hall) was, at the commencement of this action and now, the owner of the real estate described in the suit." The court documents go on:

> The plaintiff (Frank H. Hall) is in exclusive possession of said property and every portion thereof; that the defendants…have no estate, right, title, claim, or interest in and to said property, or any part thereof; that the title of the plaintiff…is quieted as against the said defendants,…and the said defendants…are hereby forever enjoined, debarred and, restrained from bringing any action against the plaintiff's title or possession of said real property, and from asserting any claim whatsoever in and to said property adverse to the plaintiff.

That Christmas of 1928, Ethel was finally able to buy presents for her children. By then, there was no mention of any expectation of presents from their father, by any of the children except Melvel. One day not long before Christmas, Melvel quietly asked Ethel if his father were to send Christmas presents, would he know to send them to California. Ethel was pleased to be able to reassure Melvel that even though there would be no presents from their father, they were going to have a happy Christmas this year. Not only did she buy a Christmas present for each of her children; she was also able to buy a cow. Ethel was tired, but she was proud of her accomplishments. She was providing for her children, and now they would even have milk.

Ethel was also proud that Robert, Jessie, and Melvel were attending school in Fairfield, most of the time. But at the end of February, the cannery work began to grind to a halt. And just as soon as Blanch and Ruby knew that they could safely travel, they too returned to Andrix. They would be going back to Arkansas soon.

When her mother and sister left Fairfield, Ethel decided that she and the children would go back to Petaluma. She could always return to Fairfield when the canning season started again. She was hopeful that she would find work in Petaluma, where she would be close to Harley and Sis. So in April 1929, Ethel sold the cow, and with Blackbird filled with kids and chickens, she moved back to Petaluma.

Harley and Sis welcomed Ethel and her children back into their home, and Ethel began searching the newspaper for work. It took some time, but one day she read that jobs were available at a prune orchard near Petaluma, twenty miles from Harley and Sis's home. She and the children headed there immediately. The orchard's trees grew a variety of plums that were specifically grown to be dried into prunes. Robert, now thirteen, was allowed to work in the orchard. Jessie's job was to watch after Melvel, Margie, and Dortha, while Ethel and Robert spent the days picking plums throughout the 1929 picking season. Each night that summer, Ethel and Robert slept on pallets on the ground near the car. Jessie, Melvel, Margie, and Dortha slept in the car. They did all their cooking over a campfire. Ethel tried to make a game of it, but it was a difficult and dirty summer for all of them.

When the prune-picking season came to an end in August, Ethel had to again make a decision. This time it was easy: she and the children would return to the rock house at Andrix. Ethel dreaded another Colorado winter, but at least she had a house and family there. And best of all, the children were very happy when she told them that they were going home. This time, the chickens stayed in Petaluma.

Ethel and the kids were back in Andrix by the end of August. They returned with the money they needed to get them through another

Colorado prairie winter, and some to spare. By the beginning of the fall school term of 1929, Robert, Jessie, and Melvel were ready to start another year at the Prairie Star School. Margie, who turned six in September, would join them, entering the first grade.

Ethel was glad to once again be close to her family, although soon after she got back to Andrix, Emil and Lola, with their five-year-old daughter Margie, moved to Dalhart, Texas. Emil was getting into the trucking business and had found an opportunity to do trucking for the railroad in Texas. Mae and Dan had also left Colorado. Dan had decided to quit the coal-mining business and return to wheat farming. They moved to Alva, Oklahoma. The Atchison, Topeka and Santa Fe Railway ran through Alva, which was therefore an area of Oklahoma where cattle ranching and wheat farming were thriving. Ethel's sister Sue and her husband, Bill Priddy, had also moved away from the Kim area. They were now living in Vernon, Texas, near Bill's parents. And Creed, Blanch, and Ruby had been back in Berryville, Arkansas, for almost three months. Now the only families left in Colorado were Claude and his children, Otto and his family, and Ethel and her children.

After Ethel returned to Andrix, she spent most of her time at Claude's homestead, helping Claude with his three older children. She and Claude had ten children between them, but by this time, Claude's twin boys, Roy and Raymond, were being cared for by Garfield Rhodes and his wife, in Pritchett, Colorado. The Winfrey treadle sewing machine was still at Claude's claim, so Ethel spent her first days back making school clothes for the seven school-aged children.

The weather on the prairie that summer had been bad. There had been little relief from the drought that had plagued the area for the past two years, and the wind seemed to blow even harder. On the afternoon of August 25, 1929, the sky darkened suddenly, and threatening clouds appeared on the horizon. Everyone became hopeful that they were finally going to get a good rain.

During the early part of the storm, tragedy struck the Winfrey family—again. As the storm approached, everyone in the Andrix area began to hustle to secure things that could possibly be blown away.

Otto left his house to put the chickens in the henhouse. As he approached the henhouse, a bolt of lightning was drawn to the structure's metal roof. It struck not only the henhouse, but Otto too, killing him instantly. Once again, the Winfreys had become victims of the harsh prairie conditions.

Creed, Blanch, and Ruby came back to Andrix, and the family gathered to mourn their loss. Otto was buried in the Kim cemetery, alongside his son Ralph. After Otto's death, his wife Valeria moved into the home of her parents, near Kim, with her two sons, Laverne and Murrel. Laverne was four years old and Murrel was fourteen months old when their father died.

Not long after Otto's death, the *Kim-Country Record* began reporting that stock market prices were falling. The paper was full of these stories every week. On Tuesday, October 29, 1929, the stock market didn't just fall—it crashed. That day, which became known as Black Tuesday, marked the beginning of what would soon be called the Great Depression. Ethel read the horror stories of the Depression in the *Kim-Country Record*, but she didn't know how anyone could be more "depressed" than they were in Colorado.

And she had no idea that the land she was living on, the land she thought was titled to Lee, had been "quiet" titled to Frank H. Hall almost a year earlier.

CHAPTER 13

1930 to 1934: The Dirty Thirties

ETHEL AND THE CHILDREN MADE IT THROUGH ANOTHER COLORADO winter in the rock house, but it was not easy. Their wood supply lasted through February, but in early March it became clear that they would not have enough wood to keep the house warm until spring. When the firewood first started to get low, Robert, without hesitation, began gathering the things he would need to go to the cedars. The need for Robert to go for more wood before the start of spring was something Ethel was trying her best to avoid, but their wood supply was becoming dangerously low, and there was no sign that winter would, by some miracle, end early.

Even though Ethel had a car, it was still essential to have a horse and wagon. Water had to be hauled, and wood had to be cut and brought home. Robert had been doing most of this work for quite some time. Ethel had retrieved Lee's wagon from Creed's homestead, and Claude had given her a horse, named Babe. Reluctantly, she and Robert decided that he had to go. The possibility that Robert could be caught in one of those sudden prairie blizzards was frightening to Ethel, but they had to have wood. Robert hitched Babe to the wagon and left at daylight the next morning—alone. He was thirteen years old.

Robert was surprised at how much faster he could travel by himself. When all the men traveled together, it was often slow and cumbersome. He followed the well-known road, Highway 109, north toward Higbee. Before dark, he found a good patch of scrub cedars and began building a fire and making his camp. The next day, he was up early, cutting cedarwood with a saw and axe and loading it into the wagon. It was cold, but the hard work kept him warm. On the second night, after he had built his campfire and eaten a bit of the food his mother had packed for him, he rolled into his blankets to sleep. He had no idea how long he had been asleep when he heard Babe rare up and begin to run. The horse had been spooked by a wild prairie animal that had run close to his camp. Babe bolted out onto the prairie, snapping the reins from the scrub bush Robert had tied her to. Robert, knowing he absolutely could not lose that horse, jumped up and began running after her in his bare feet—he didn't have time to put on his boots. The moon was bright, and he had good vision. Babe ran and ran, and so did Robert. Finally, Babe tired, and Robert was able to catch up to her. He had gotten the horse, but not without injuries to his feet. They were badly cut and bleeding. Yet a disaster had been averted.

Robert spent another day, crippled but determined, filling the wagon with cedarwood, and then he went home. The day he returned was one of Ethel's happiest. The entire time he was gone, she had prayed fervently that he would be safe. Her prayers had been answered. Now they would make it through the winter.

By the start of 1930, Claude's twin sons, Roy and Raymond, were still being cared for by the Rhodes family in Pritchett, Colorado, twenty-five miles east of Andrix. But in April of that year, Roy developed polio and died. Irene, who was thirteen at the time, wrote about the death of her brother in *Irene and Levi, Our Journey Through Life*:

> *The twins lived with the Rhodes family until Roy took Infantile Paralysis, later called Polio. He died April 2, 1930 near the age of two. Dad and Mr. and Mrs. Rhodes took his casket in the back seat of our car to Rosston, Oklahoma where my mother is buried. Polio left Roy paralyzed on his left side. I missed my baby brother so much and had already resigned to take care of him the rest of my life.*
>
> *When Dad came back from Oklahoma, he decided that we could take care of Raymond, and we brought him home.... We went to school with Raymond, all of us Creeda, Ben, Raymond and I, even though Raymond was only two years old. We lived a half mile from school and*

I carried Raymond there every day. The teacher, Mr. Freeman, was so good to let us bring him to school. Raymond was so good and real quiet while the rest of us kids studied. I've always appreciated Mr. Freeman for letting us take Raymond to school.

Robert turned fourteen in March 1930, and that spring, Ethel and Robert were determined to once again try to grow a garden. There was a small amount of rainfall in May, and by hauling some water from the stream that continued to run through the claim, they were able to grow some beans. But what they grew was not nearly enough to get them through another long winter. Ethel still had most of the money she and Robert had made picking plums. She had been trying her best to save it for as long as possible, but in order to have enough food for the winter, she would have to go to Kim for supplies.

By 1930, Kim and the surrounding area had grown to a population of about seven hundred. The Kim commercial district now had three general merchandise stores, two cafés, three gas stations, a barbershop, a bank, a cobbler shop, a drugstore, a hotel, tourist cabins, and the *Kim-Country Record* newspaper office. As Ethel drove to Kim, she tried to remember what the little community had looked like when she and Lee had arrived with their youthful plans to start a new and exciting life together—and to have 320 acres of land that would be all theirs. She could hardly believe that fourteen years had passed since then.

While in Kim that day, a fortunate opportunity presented itself to Ethel. That summer of 1930, despite the drought, Kim had begun experiencing a housing shortage. To meet the growing demand for houses, a local contractor had bought the houses of a closed mining district near Trinidad. He had disassembled the houses and transported them in pieces to Kim, where he was reconstructing and selling them. The houses were small, but they were somewhat insulated and very affordable. Ethel, seeing an opportunity to have a warmer house for her children, managed somehow to buy one of the houses. She had it put up on the claim near the rock house, which became the barn. Finally, she had a house above ground that would be easier to keep warm. She was still completely unaware that the land she was living on, and had now built a house on, had been titled to someone she did not know, a year and a half earlier.

There was a good deal of Winfrey family news throughout the year of 1930. Blanch continued to faithfully send her weekly letters. Her mid-April letter happily reported that Ruby had married Verne M. Royse in Berryville, on April 2, 1930—the same day that Claude's son Roy had died. Toward the end of that April, Blanch wrote that Emil and Lola had had another daughter, Ardith Emilline Winfrey, born on April 26, 1930, in Dalhart, Texas. Another letter from Blanch reported that Gertie and Bennett's daughter Mildred, who was now eighteen years old, was going to college. She was the first member of the Creed Winfrey family to attend college. Gertie and Bennett were still living on their farm near Braymer, Missouri.

AND…the 1930 census shows that Lee, Bessie, and Billie (William C.) were living in Flagstaff, Arizona. Billie was eight years old. Also listed as living with them was a girl named Sarah Lecero. She was sixteen and was listed as their maid. Lee recorded his occupation as mercantile salesman.

Robert went to the cedars with Claude that fall and returned home with plenty of wood to get them through the winter. As soon as he returned, he started the eighth grade at the Prairie Star School. It would be his last year of school. Jessie was eleven and started the fifth grade; Melvel was nine and started the fourth grade; and Margie, who turned seven in September, started the second grade.

Despite the dry conditions, Andrix, like Kim, was continuing to grow—a little. By this time, a school had been built and opened next to the Andrix store. Claude's children Irene, Creeda, and Benjamin began attending the Andrix school as soon as it opened. It was the Andrix schoolteacher who allowed them to bring their baby brother Raymond to school with them. Ethel missed Erma, Claude's wife, more than she would admit even to herself, but she also missed her mother and father, terribly. She was able to see Valeria, Otto's widow, occasionally, but those occasions seemed to be getting fewer and further between. She was beginning to accept that none of her family would ever return to Andrix. Harley and Sis were sending letters saying that they intended to stay in Petaluma, and now, with Ruby married to a man from Berryville, there was little hope that her mother and father would ever return to Andrix. Thankfully, Claude had every intention of staying, so at least she was not there completely alone. But the isolation that had affected her mother so much was beginning to wear on Ethel as well.

When the cold weather started that October, Ethel was extremely worried. She had cornmeal, milk, beans, and a few laying hens, but little else, and she had spent most of her money on the wooden house. She still had her Quaker friends, who always helped her. But sometimes she and the children were not able to leave the house for extended periods of time, because of the winter storms. She was very aware that she must ration their food supply—just in case. The most important thing was to have something for the children to take to school for lunch. There were many days that winter when the only meal they had was the cornbread that she packed in each of their school bags. That Christmas, she killed one of their hens, and they had fried chicken for their Christmas dinner. That was the best gift she could give them.

By now, none of the children, not even Melvel, talked of any possibility of receiving Christmas gifts from their father. In fact, Ethel noticed that they no longer talked about him at all. It was just as well. She was sure that the next time she heard from him would be when she received papers notifying her that he had filed for divorce. Those papers never came.

Ethel had raised her children to kneel beside their beds each night and thank God for his blessings. They always found something to be thankful for. But this winter was different. This winter, they all knelt beside their beds each night and prayed for their next meal. Despite their dire circumstances, Ethel always had faith that God would take care of them, and that he would give her the strength to do whatever needed to be done.

Somehow, they made it through that tough winter. In March 1931, Robert turned fifteen, and in May he graduated from the eighth grade. They went to Claude's homestead to have a little family celebration; Irene had also graduated from the eighth grade, so they celebrated together. A high school had opened in Kim by this time, but Robert knew that going to high school was not an option for him. His mother needed him too much—he was the man of the family.

That March, of 1931, the newspapers all over Colorado, and all over the United States, began reporting on a terrible weather-related incident that had occurred just a few miles north of Lamar. Ethel was horrified by the newspaper accounts of the tragedy. On March 26, 1931, a rural school bus had picked up twenty children who lived on the Colorado prairie around the communities of Towner and Holly. By the time the bus arrived at the Pleasant Hill School, it had started to snow, and the skies were dark. Because the school was not prepared to house the children for an extended length of time, the decision was made to load the children back onto the bus and take them home. It was snowing hard by the time the bus was on its way, and within minutes, it was caught in a complete prairie whiteout. The bus driver did his best to follow fence lines, but eventually the bus slid into a ditch, and the engine died.

The bus—a 1929 Chevrolet truck that had been turned into a school bus by attaching a wooden body to the truck bed—was not heated and had broken windows. It provided very little shelter from the blizzard conditions; the wind blew the snow sideways and into the bus through the broken windows. The children and the driver spent the rest of the day and night in the bus. The temperature dropped to twenty degrees below zero, and the wind blew up to seventy miles an hour. At daybreak, the driver, knowing that the children were freezing and near death, left the bus in an attempt to find help.

The parents had no idea that their children were stranded in the snow-covered bus. They were sure they were safe in the schoolhouse. The next morning, some parents managed to get to the school, only to find out that the children were not there. The search began.

The children were in the bus for thirty-three hours before they were found. Five children froze to death—including the bus driver's daughter—and the driver's frozen body was found about three and a half miles from the bus. The surviving children were taken to the Charles Maxwell Hospital in Lamar. The newspapers called the horrifying catastrophe the Towner Bus Tragedy. Within days, the entire country knew of the disaster.

The tragedy had an enormous impact on Ethel. Being caught out in a prairie blizzard was something she always feared, and this tragic event proved just how bad it could be. Once again, she thought of possibly leaving Colorado. But she didn't know where to go or what to do, so she stayed.

In the fall of 1931, the children returned to the Prairie Star School. That year, Dortha turned six and started the first grade. Jessie was in the sixth grade, Melvel in fifth, and Margie in third. Robert stayed home and helped his mother.

Irene started high school that fall. She described her high school experience in chapter 10 of *Irene and Levi, Our Journey Through Life*:

> *I entered High School at Kim and rode the school bus with Mr. Bennett as the driver. He drove the bus for several school terms. I went to High School one and a half years and had to quit because times were hard and I did not have clothes good enough to wear to school. Mrs. Garfield Rhoades made me three dresses my freshman year of school. Two were dresses for school and one for everyday wear. Washing and ironing them every week, they soon became faded and worn, so I quit school. This was the last of my schooling.*

The national news of 1931 was mostly about the Depression. Times were difficult, and people were hungry. The unemployment rate was rising every day, and soup kitchens in large cities were overwhelmed. But one positive thing that captured everyone's attention was the completion of the Empire State Building in New York City. Despite the Depression, the building had been erected in thirteen months, providing badly needed jobs for a lot of men.

At the beginning of the spring of 1932, Robert told Ethel that he would do whatever it took to grow a good crop that year. He said he would haul water every day if that was what it would take. He turned sixteen that March, but to Ethel it seemed as though he were thirty. Together they planted a big garden—with plenty of help from all the children. Because of the drought, the little stream that ran through the claim was beginning to dry up. Robert eventually had to take the wagon to Claude's claim for water. Claude had a windmill that pumped water, and Robert would fill two barrels: one for the family and one for irrigation. Robert and Ethel were beginning to see a worrisome difference in the drought-plagued topsoil. After being plowed, it was easily blown away by the severe winds that seemed to be occurring more and more often.

Yet they were able to bring in some crops that season, and it looked as if they would have enough to make it through another winter. And their chicken coop was filled with chickens. They were doing okay—for a change.

In September 1932, Jessie, Melvel, Margie, and Dortha started school at the Prairie Star School. Ethel was proud that she was able to keep her children in school. Jessie was in the seventh grade, and Robert began talking about the possibility of Jessie going to high school in Kim after she finished the eighth grade.

By that fall the dust was starting to blow every day. There were times when it was impossible to go outside, and there were many days when Ethel decided that the kids could not go to school because the dust storms were so bad.

There was other important national news throughout the year of 1932. It was an election year, and Franklin Roosevelt, the governor of New York, was running against President Herbert Hoover. There seemed to be no end in sight for the Great Depression, and Roosevelt blamed Hoover for the worsening economy. Roosevelt ran on a promise of economic recovery with his New Deal for the American people. He won by a landslide on Tuesday, November 8, 1932.

The year 1933 started out with news of the launching of Roosevelt's New Deal. One part of the New Deal was the formation of the Civil Works Administration (CWA), a job-creation program established to rapidly provide manual-labor jobs to millions of unemployed workers. Ethel and Robert read about the CWA with the hopes that it would provide work in their area of Colorado. Roosevelt also supported the repeal of Prohibition. Prohibition had been in effect since 1920, and many Americans believed that it had not only *not* ended drinking but had diminished respect for the law and fostered a massive bootlegging industry.

Ethel and Robert did not have to wait long for news about possible CWA work projects in the Kim area. In August, the *Kim-Country Record* reported that small projects in and around Kim were being planned and applied for. The projects were designed to give immediate, short-term jobs to unemployed men throughout the winter of 1933–1934. The next edition of the paper reported that the first CWA project had been approved. A teacher's living quarters and a horse shelter would be built for the Prairie Star School. Work would begin within weeks. Men could apply for work at the Kim post office. Robert went to apply right away. He received word by mail that he could begin work on the Prairie Star School structure in September. He was seventeen years old.

In September 1933, Jessie, Melvel, Margie, and Dortha all started school at the Prairie Star School, and Robert started work—also at the Prairie Star School. Jessie was in the eighth grade, Melvel the seventh, Margie the fifth, and Dortha the third. Ethel was, for the first time in years, not so worried about the oncoming winter. She now knew that they would be fine and would probably never be hungry again—because of Robert.

The Winfrey family had another occasion to celebrate in November of that year. Claude's daughter Irene married Levi Jones. Irene wrote about her marriage to Levi in chapter 12 of *Irene and Levi, Our Journey Through Life*:

> *Levi and I met in the Spring and November 16, 1933 we were married. Looking back over those "dirty thirties", when the wind and dirt was blowing clouds of dust day after day, I wondered how Levi and I had the courage to get married and start a family. Times were really hard and jobs were hard to find. We were married by the Justice of the Peace at Springfield and had a total of two dollars when we got home. After we were married we stayed with Dad and Levi snapped corn*

through the winter. I cooked for my father and the boys and kept house for all of us. That was the last good crop we raised for several years.

The Prairie Star School building project was finished by the end of November, but fortunately, by that time, another CWA project was underway. Approval had been given for the building of a school gymnasium in Kim, and the work would begin in December. As soon as this was announced, Robert went to get a job working on the gymnasium. A bunkhouse, referred to as "the shack," was put up first to house the CWA workers who did not live in Kim. Since Robert lived seven miles from Kim, he was given a bunk in the shack. The gymnasium work was sporadic and between jobs, he would return home. He was notified, by courier, each time work that they needed him for resumed. Robert worked off and on in Kim throughout the rest of the winter. He made about eighteen dollars a month.

Ethel received a letter from Mae at the end of 1933. Mae and Dan had moved again. They had left Alva, Oklahoma, and had bought a farm in the Hico section of Siloam Springs, Arkansas. Siloam Springs was just across the Oklahoma-Arkansas state line, about 270 miles from Alva. Mae wrote of nothing but praises for Siloam Springs. Her letter said that it was a flourishing little town in a beautiful area of Arkansas, a stop on the Kansas City Southern Railroad. She ended her letter with a short note about John Brown College, which she said was the best thing about Siloam Springs. She was excited that Kenneth, now twenty-three, and Mary, now eighteen, would both be attending John Brown College.

The winter months of the new year of 1934 were dry and long. There was no rain and very little snow, but as usual, it was extremely cold. It seemed to Ethel that Robert was in Kim more than he was home, but she was grateful for his opportunities to work. When spring finally arrived, Robert came home long enough to plant some crops, but conditions were worsening with the drought and the continual dust storms. It was beginning to look as though it would be almost impossible to grow much of anything—maybe some beans, but nothing else. And to make matters worse, Ethel and Claude received letters from Blanch telling them that their father was not well.

That March, Robert turned eighteen, and in May Jessie graduated from the eighth grade. Robert's CWA work continued; he was still earning about eighteen dollars a month.

As the weather warmed, the *Kim-Country Record* began to report frequent stories about the dust storms. With each story, the situation appeared to be growing increasingly serious. The dust was hitting Oklahoma hard, and people were pouring out of that state and heading for California. People were also beginning to leave the Kim-Andrix area. Ethel was worried. Irene wrote about the dust storms in chapter 12 of *Irene and Levi, Our Journey Through Life*:

> *The year of 1934 was a real bad year, it was so dry (and no winter moisture) that we could not farm for ourselves, so Levi found work driving a tractor for a farmer west of Pritchett. They had a little winter moisture when we did not get any. This job did not last long because it got so dry and the ground so hard that the lister would not go into the ground…. Keep in mind these years I am speaking of, the wind and dirt is still blowing and no winter moisture at all, so people could not get the crops planted. There was not enough moisture to sprout the seed, much less for the seed to grow. Clouds and clouds of dust, like smoke would rise up in the north and when it hit we would have to light our coal oil lamps in the daytime. I really dreaded to see those awful clouds of dust banking up in the north and bearing down on us. There were several people who died of dust pneumonia.*

It was on May 9, 1934, that the worst dust storm hit. Everyone on the Great Plains had to stay in their houses for days. Newspapers across the country reported that the storm removed an estimated three hundred million tons of fertile topsoil from the Great Plains. After that storm, Ethel knew there was no chance of growing anything to eat that year. There seemed to be no relief from the constant dust in sight. She didn't know what they would do, but if Robert's job with the CWA ended, they would have to leave.

When the CWA was approved by Congress, it had been funded for only a short period of time. Sometime during the latter part of 1934, the funds began to be depleted, and Robert's work opportunities slowed down. The people of Kim attempted to raise money to keep the work on the gymnasium going, but it was slow.

CHAPTER 14

1935: Potato Soup

THROUGHOUT THE YEAR OF 1934, BLANCH'S WEEKLY LETTERS continued; each one reported that Creed, now seventy-eight, was still not doing well. Ethel and Claude grew more concerned and began to talk about a possible trip to Arkansas for a funeral. Claude began making daily trips to the telegraph office in Kim. On December 3, the telegram arrived. Creed had died that morning.

Mae and Dan were still living in Siloam Springs, Arkansas, eighty miles from Berryville. Mae sent a telegram to Ethel telling her to come to Siloam Springs. They would go to Berryville together for their father's funeral. It would be on Thursday, December 6.

Ethel and Claude started making plans immediately. They would take the train from Lamar to Siloam Springs. Ethel wanted Robert to go to Arkansas with her, so it was decided—the three younger children, Melvel (thirteen), Margie (eleven), and Dortha (nine), would stay on the claim under the care of Jessie, now fifteen. Ethel and Robert would be gone for six days.

Ethel quickly began preparing for the trip. As she packed, she told Jessie that Melvel, Margie, and Dortha would not be going to school that week. She wanted Jessie to keep them at the house while she and Robert were gone. She told them all that if it snowed, they were to walk to the outdoor toilet together. She emphasized again and again that if it snowed, no one was to walk to the outhouse alone. Claude, Ethel, and Robert left early on Tuesday, December 4.

The children spent that first day trying to entertain themselves in and around the house, and keeping the fire going in the stove to stay warm. It was mid-afternoon when there was a knock on the door. A courier for the Kim gymnasium CWA project was there to deliver a work notice for Robert. Jessie took the notice and opened it quickly. It said that Robert was needed, and he should come to Kim as soon as possible. Jessie, knowing that this opportunity would be lost because Robert was in Arkansas, decided that Melvel would have to go in Robert's place. It was money they had to have. She told them all to start getting ready: they would be going to Kim the next day.

The next morning, they were all up early, excited about going to Kim. Melvel had no idea what he would be doing, but he tried his best to get ready for whatever it might be. As soon as they were all ready to go, Jessie went out to start the car. She had driven it many times, but she had never actually started it herself. She was sure she could do it. She tried and tried, but the car would not start. She finally gave up; they would have to walk. Robert's work opportunities were becoming fewer and further apart, and Jessie was determined that they weren't going to miss this one. She instructed them all to put on the warmest clothes they had. By midmorning, they were on their way.

Walking to the Andrix store was something they did often. It was two and a half miles from their claim. In warm weather, some of them would usually ride Babe, while the others walked. Jessie knew very well that their mother would never let them walk to the store in the dead of winter, but this trip to Kim was just too important—they had to go. It was very cold, but the sky was clear, and they made it to the road that went from Kim to Andrix in good time and without any difficulty. At that road, they turned right toward Kim and kept walking. Jessie knew, when they got to the road, that they had walked two miles, and Kim was five miles away. She was sure they could get there, find the CWA shack where Melvel would stay, and get back home before dark. But when they had walked about another mile, dark clouds moved over the road ahead. It started to snow. Jessie was worried about the sudden snowfall, but she was determined that they should keep going. By now, it was almost as far to get back home as it was to Kim.

It was getting colder, and the snow kept coming, heavier every minute. After about another mile and a lot more snow, Jessie began to worry that they may be in trouble. Margie and Dortha were having difficulty walking and were starting to say how cold they were. Melvel was trying to be brave, but he was slowing down too. Jessie, not knowing what else to do, insisted that they keep going. Kim had to be less than three miles away.

Eventually she relented and let them stop to rest. It was becoming obvious to both Jessie and Melvel that they were in the middle of one of those prairie blizzard whiteouts. The thing that worried Jessie the most was that they had not seen anyone else on the road the entire day.

It was when Jessie told them that they had to keep walking that they began to faintly see a wagon coming toward them through the heavy snow. It took a while, but finally the wagon pulled up and stopped. It was another homesteader, Luther Botts, whom they knew from church. That day, Luther loaded four exhausted, shivering, and hungry children into his wagon. He knew where their home was, and he told them he would try to take them there. But the snow kept getting worse, and the best he could do was take them to the home of Fred and Icie Cox, the people who had bought the Andrix store from Harley. They lived in the back of the store.

By the time they arrived at the Andrix store, it was getting late, and the snow was still coming down. It was quickly decided that the children would stay with Fred and Icie that night. They would decide the next day if the children could go home. Jessie was still determined to get Melvel to Kim, and she told them that they would try to walk there the next day. Luther told her that if at all possible, he would return to the store and take them to Kim.

That night, Fred, Icie, and their four sons shared their pot of potato soup with the Bailey children and gave them a place to sleep. That soup was remembered by all of them—for the rest of their lives—as the absolute best potato soup they ever had.

The next day, the weather warmed, and by that afternoon Luther had returned. He was able to take them to Kim in his wagon. The only person they found at the CWA shack was the work supervisor; all the other workers had been sent home because of the snow. Jessie told the supervisor that Melvel was there to take Robert's place. The supervisor replied that Melvel could not work—he was too young. Luther, who had known that this would probably be the case, took them home. They stayed at home, safe and warm—thanks to Luther Botts and Fred and Icie Cox—until Ethel and Robert returned.

By the time Ethel and Robert got home from their journey to Creed's funeral, they had made a big decision. After the funeral, Mae had insisted on showing Ethel and Robert the beautiful little town of Siloam Springs, and she especially wanted to take them to the John Brown College (now called John Brown University) campus. Mae couldn't say enough good things about Siloam Springs—primarily because of the university. Mae told Ethel and Robert about the school. It had been started several years earlier by John E. Brown Sr. as an interdenominational Christian vocational school. John Brown's intent was to provide a school where disadvantaged students, who might not have a chance to get an education, could pay for their education by working for the school while they attended classes. Mae was excited about the fact that there was a high school as well as a college on the campus. She told Ethel that there was a possibility that all her children could finish high school and attend college at John Brown University, by working for the college to pay their tuition.

Ethel had never dreamed of such a thing, and Robert saw an opportunity for the other children to get a high school diploma. For Ethel, the possibility of her children being able to work their way through a Christian education was something she wanted to at least give them the opportunity for. Ethel and Robert decided, with Mae's encouragement, to move to the Siloam Springs area. Their minds were made up: they would leave the dust-stricken Colorado prairie and move to Arkansas. And it couldn't happen fast enough.

When Ethel and Robert arrived home and found out about the walk to Kim, they started making plans to move immediately. They were finished with the hard Colorado winters and the dust storms—it was time to leave. Ethel sent a letter to Emil to ask him if he could help her move. Emil was now in Kiowa, Kansas, still in the trucking business. Emil's return letter told her to start preparing to move; he and his father-in-law, Wiley Winters, would bring two trucks to Andrix. They would be there with the first signs of spring.

In March 1935, Robert turned nineteen, and Jessie turned sixteen in April. Melvel turned fourteen in May and graduated from the eighth grade at the Prairie Star School. Margie finished the sixth grade, and Dortha finished the fourth grade.

Despite all the moving plans and excitement, Robert decided that he would not go to Arkansas right away. Instead, he would stay on the claim site and attempt to bring in one more crop, and hopefully work some on the Kim gymnasium. It was a big decision for Ethel, but Robert made it easy for her. They didn't know what was ahead of them once they got to Arkansas, so it only made sense for Robert to stay on the claim and attempt to bring in a crop. Maybe he could at least grow some beans—beans that may be badly needed in Arkansas. Also, there had been news that the CWA work on the Kim gymnasium was going to be resumed under the new Works Progress Administration (WPA), another program in Roosevelt's New Deal plan.

It was all planned: Ethel would drive Blackbird with the children, while Emil and Wiley would haul their horse, Babe, and all their belongings in their two trucks. Robert would stay in Colorado and move to Arkansas before winter.

Since Siloam Springs was right on the Oklahoma-Arkansas state line, Ethel wrote to Mae suggesting that they move close to Siloam Springs, but actually live in Oklahoma, just across the state line. Mae began looking for a place for Ethel to rent, and soon she found a house in the small community of Flint, Oklahoma. Because of the difficult times brought on by the Depression, Harry McClelland, the owner of the house, was willing to move into his barn in order to rent his house. Ethel sent Mae a letter telling her to inform Mr. McClelland that they would be there in June.

When Emil and Wiley arrived in Andrix ready to move Ethel and the children, Emil had a surprise for Ethel. During one of his hauling trips, he had gone through Flagstaff, Arizona, and had paid Lee a visit. Lee was not at all pleased to see him, but Emil told him, frankly, that he was there "just to collect." Lee gave Emil some money to take to Ethel. Emil let Lee know that it wasn't enough, but Lee said it was the best he could do. Ethel was grateful for her brother's concern and determination. It was badly needed money, and she was extremely happy to get it.

By the end of May, everything was loaded into Emil's trucks except for the few things Robert would need to stay on the claim. Emil was willing to haul Babe to Oklahoma, but he said that someone would have to ride in the back of the truck with the horse, in order to keep her calm and under control. That assignment was given to Jessie—she was the oldest. Jessie didn't like the idea, but she was willing to do anything to get out of Colorado.

Ethel and the kids said their good-byes to Robert, and they started their journey to Flint. As they left, Ethel looked back at the dugout that she and Lee had built; the rock house that she, Lee, and her brothers had built; and the wooden house that she had managed to have put up on the claim. With a sense of accomplishment, she told the children that they would, most assuredly, never return.

As they pulled away, Jessie, in the back of the truck with Babe, felt a glimmer of hopeful anticipation as to what might lie ahead. As she watched her childhood home fade into the distance, she promised herself that she would try to forget, and she would never again talk about what would soon be in the past.

Robert waved good-bye and immediately set to work on another impossible garden. A few days later, on May 6, 1935, President Roosevelt signed the executive order that initiated the WPA. It wasn't long before Robert got the notice that work on the Kim gymnasium had begun again.

Robert worked on the Kim gymnasium and attempted to grow some crops. But because of the continuous dust, it was not only impossible to grow any crops; it was almost impossible to make headway on the Kim gymnasium. The work on the gymnasium continued nonetheless—slowly.

CHAPTER 15

Flint, Oklahoma: The Last New Beginning

IT TOOK ALMOST THREE FULL DAYS TO ARRIVE IN FLINT. ETHEL FOUND the house that Mae had located. It was still available and awaiting their arrival. With Emil and Wiley's help, they moved in. It was, once again, a brand-new start.

Once they were settled in, Ethel encouraged Jessie to go to the John Brown University campus in Siloam Springs and ask to see Dr. Brown. She told Jessie to tell Dr. Brown that she had no money, but she wanted to work her way through high school. Jessie didn't waste any time. She arose early one morning and started the thirteen-mile walk from Flint to Siloam Springs. That day, Dr. Brown enrolled Jessie in high school, found a place for her to live and work on campus, and provided her with the books she would need. Her walk back to Flint was more of a run than a walk. She was anxious to tell her mother that she was going to high school, and she knew that, thanks to Dr. Brown, she was now beginning the only life she wanted to remember.

That September, Margie started the seventh grade at the Flint School, and Dortha started the fifth grade. Jessie was the only one of Ethel's children to attend John Brown Academy, and to graduate from high school.

Back in Colorado, Robert was unable to grow anything in the dust-covered garden. After working in Kim on the gymnasium that summer, he packed up his duffel bag in order to head out for Oklahoma before the cold weather. As he was going through the house, gathering up the things he would take with him, he found Melvel's leg brace, stuffed away in a pile of rags. He laughed at the thought of his mother never being willing to throw anything away—not rags, and not a brace made for a three-year-old child. He sat down and looked at the brace, remembering what a difficult time Melvel had had learning to walk in it. It brought back memories that he really didn't want to remember. Knowing that the brace would never be used again, but not wanting to put it in the trash, Robert slid it between the walls of the wooden house. Then he picked up his duffel bag and started walking to the Andrix store, where he would flag down the bus that now ran between Kim and Springfield. He was on his way to Oklahoma.

EPILOGUE

Ethel: After Ethel and her children got to Flint, Oklahoma, their lives began to slowly normalize. Ethel lived near Flint throughout World War II. Both of her sons, Robert and Melvel, and all three of her sons-in-law were called into active service, and all returned home safely. Robert was the only one to serve overseas.

Not long after the move to Flint, Ethel learned, probably through Emil, that Lee was living in San Bernardino, California. Emil always managed to somehow keep up with Lee. In 1940, five years after they left Colorado, Robert took Ethel, Margie, and Dortha to San Bernardino to find Lee. Margie was seventeen years old, and Dortha was fifteen. Their mission was to confront him about the oil, gas, and mineral rights to the Colorado claim. After locating Lee's place of business (probably an automobile-parts store) in San Bernardino, Robert walked into the store and asked Lee, "Is your last name Bailey?" When Lee said that it was, Robert said, "Well, so is mine." It was undoubtedly at this meeting that Ethel learned that Lee had given up the title to the land; the land she had lived on until 1935 had been "quiet" titled to a complete stranger in 1928.

Ethel spent the rest of her life living near all her children except Melvel. Melvel lived in California, but he stayed close to his mother and all of his siblings. In January 1947, after her children helped her get a divorce from Lee, Ethel married Hiram A. Whetzel. She died on May 16, 1987, at the age of ninety-two. She is buried in the Allen Cemetery in West Siloam Springs, Oklahoma.

Robert: Robert married the one and only love of his life, Grace Barnett, in 1941. Grace was from the Flint, Oklahoma, area. Robert and Grace had one son, whom they raised in the Flint, Oklahoma / Siloam Springs, Arkansas, area. Robert served in World War II as a sergeant in the US Army. After basic training at Sheppard Field in Texas, he was sent to the South Pacific, where he fought in the horrific battles of Saipan and Okinawa. After the war, he built a house in Siloam Springs for his mother and operated a successful construction company, building many homes in and around Siloam Springs. He was *always* near his mother, until his early death at age sixty-six, in 1983. Ethel outlived her beloved Robert; she was eighty-eight when Robert died. Robert was buried in the Allen Cemetery in West Siloam Springs, Oklahoma. Ethel joined him there four years later.

Melvel: Melvel also met his wife in the Flint, Oklahoma, area. He married JoAda Robinson, who was from Watts, Oklahoma, in March 1942. Melvel served as a private in the US Army in World War II and was called into active service six months after he and JoAda were married. In 1947, Melvel and JoAda made the decision to move to San Bernardino, California, where Melvel knew his father was living. By then, Lee and Bessie had been living in San Bernardino for at least eleven years, and Lee had become successful in the real estate business. Melvel made contact with his father and maintained a relationship with him until Lee's death in 1967.

After the move to San Bernardino, Melvel started the B&B Construction Company. The company's successful startup was in part a result of Lee's introduction of Melvel to influential businesspeople in San Bernardino. Based on the recollection of Melvel's daughter Donna, Bessie was never aware of Melvel and Lee's renewed relationship. After having three children, Melvel and JoAda adopted two sons. They raised their five children in San Bernardino. Melvel died just four months before his sister Jessie. He and JoAda are also buried in the Allen Cemetery in West Siloam Springs, Oklahoma, along with Ethel.

Jessie: Jessie worked in the John Brown University cafeteria and graduated high school from the John Brown Academy in 1938. She then went on to nursing school at the John Brown University Hospital.

While attending nursing school, she met and married Garland Jackson. Garland was raised in Siloam Springs, and that is where he and Jessie raised their four children. Garland passed away at the early age of fifty-four. After his death, Jessie remained in the Siloam Springs / Springdale, Arkansas, area. She married Clint Hayes in 1974. She was married to him for thirty-five years, until her death in 2009.

None of the details of this story were learned from Jessie. She always refused to talk about her childhood on the Colorado prairie. When asked, she would only say, "I was born in Kim, Colorado"; however, her birth certificate lists Andrix as her place of birth. On a family vacation to California in 1955, Melvel urged Jessie to go see their father. After finding Lee's house in San Bernardino, my mother sat in our car outside and lost her nerve—she said she couldn't do it. I remember my father telling her, "If you don't see him now, you never will." It was a difficult thing for her to do, but she did it. Bessie answered the door, and we went in. I think my mother was proud to show her father that despite his absence, she had survived, and survived well.

Margie: Margie married Daryel Ames, who was also from the Flint, Oklahoma, area, in 1939. Daryel served in the US Navy during World War II and did his basic training in San Diego, California. Margie followed Daryel to California and worked as a "Rosie the Riveter," one of the women who took men's positions during World War II in American factories and shipyards. Margie was a beautiful girl. While working in the shipyards in San Diego, she was nominated to compete in the Miss San Diego Beauty Pageant, representing the shipyard. After the war, Margie and Daryel returned to Oklahoma, where they opened a grocery store and gasoline station in Choteau. They raised their two daughters there. Ethel always lived close to Margie. The last house in which she lived was just across the highway from Margie and Daryel's store.

Dortha: Dortha met her husband, Percy Noble, in Flint, Oklahoma. She went to school with him at the Flint School. Percy (who was also called Boodle) also served in the US Navy during World War II. He was an amateur boxer and boxed in Golden Glove competitions for the navy. Dortha and Percy had three daughters after the war and spent a lot of time moving between Texas, California, and Arkansas. In California, they worked in the shipyards. When Dortha went with Ethel, Robert, and Margie to San Bernardino in 1940 to find Lee, it was the first and only time that Dortha saw her father, and the first and only time that he saw her. Dortha always stayed close to her mother.

THE REST OF THE STORY

Ethel's Mother, Brothers, and Sisters

Blanch M. Smith Winfrey: Ethel's mother, Blanch, stayed in Berryville after Creed's death. However, she spent a lot of time traveling to visit her children. She died on August 28, 1944, ten years after Creed. She is buried next to Creed in the Berryville Memorial Cemetery. Her headstone reads: "Blanch M. Winfrey 1877–1944."

Lilly Mae Winfrey Lynch: Ethel's sister Mae and her husband, Dan Lynch, spent the rest of their lives in Siloam Springs, Arkansas. They are both buried in the Oak Hill Cemetery in Siloam Springs. Their son Kenneth graduated from John Brown University with a degree in art, and he later taught art at JBU. Kenneth married Daisy May Jones. He and Daisy May did not have any children. Before Daisy May died, she shared many pieces of Kenneth's artwork with Ethel's grandchildren. Kenneth's art is proudly displayed in many of their homes.

Mae and Dan's daughter Mary Lorene Lynch also graduated from John Brown University. She married Peter J. Lindemann. After Peter graduated from dental school, they moved to Flagstaff, Arizona, where they raised their three children. Peter served one term as mayor of Flagstaff. Mary later earned a master's degree in art education from Northern Arizona University, and her name became synonymous with watercolor paintings. Her artwork gained her recognition with the Arizona and American Watercolor Associations. Mary stayed active in the art world up to the time of her death in 2007.

Gertrude Grace Winfrey Long: After Ethel's sister Gertie married Bennett Long, they lived in Missouri for the rest of their lives. She was the only one of Creed's children to stay in Missouri. According to Irene Winfrey Jones's book *Irene and Levi, Our Journey Through Life*, Gertie and Bennett made a few trips to Colorado to visit her family, but apparently she and Bennett were never tempted to move there. Irene described Gertie and Bennett's visits to Colorado:

> *I was real small when Dad's relatives from Missouri came to visit. I remember him saying that they were "well-off" and they had "white collared" jobs. At this time I wondered what "white collared" jobs were. When they arrived they looked like most people there in town. I remember so well that they would stand in our doorway and enjoyed looking as far as their eyes could see at the country.*
>
> *Missouri is so hilly that they could not see very far. Colorado was flat and a person could see for miles and miles. We kids were always anxious to have them come and visit us for they would bring black walnuts. They sent some through the mail and they tasted so good, but were so hard to crack.*

Gertie and Bennett's farm was three miles east of Braymer, Missouri. They lived on their farm until 1963, when they moved into Braymer. Braymer is only thirty-seven miles from Carrollton—she never moved far from her childhood home. Gertie died in Chillicothe, Missouri, in 1974 at age ninety, and Bennett died in 1984. He was ninety-nine. She and Bennett are both buried in the Evergreen Cemetery in Braymer. Margaret was their only child.

Claude William Winfrey: Ethel's brother Claude remained on his land around Andrix for almost the rest of his life. As the years went by, he acquired more land, and eventually he owned several 320-acre plots—possibly well over 1,000 acres. Erma's death in 1928 left Claude a single father of five children: Irene, Creeda, Ben, Raymond, and Roy. (Roy died in 1930.) Fifteen years after Erma's death, in 1943, Claude met and married Margaret Smith Davis, from Springfield, Colorado. Margaret helped care for mothers and their newborn babies in Springfield; Claude met her after the birth of his third grandchild, who was born in Springfield. Margaret and Claude were together for twenty years. Eventually they moved to La Junta, Colorado, where Claude died in

1963. He is buried in the Andrix cemetery. Margaret died twenty years after Claude and is buried next to him.

Claude and Erma's daughter Irene lived in and around the Kim-Andrix area for most of her life. After she married Levi Jones, she and Levi continued to try to farm in the Andrix area, despite the terrible dust conditions, in order to stay close to their families. Levi farmed with Claude for many years. In 1955, the sheriff of Las Animas County offered Levi the position of deputy sheriff of eastern Las Animas County. Levi was the deputy sheriff from 1955 until his death in 1971. He died of emphysema, said to be a result of cigarettes and breathing so much dust. After Levi's death, Irene moved to La Junta to be close to, and take care of, her stepmother, Margaret. In the later part of Irene's life, with the encouragement of her children, she wrote her life story. With the help of her daughter Donna Pearce, her story was published as a small paperback book, *Irene and Levi, Our Journey Through Life*, in 2007. Irene died on June 21, 2008. She is buried next to Levi in the Kim cemetery.

Harley Glen Winfrey: Once Ethel's brother Harley and his wife Viola (Sis) moved to Petaluma, California, they never left. The 1930 census shows that Harley listed his profession as poultryman, and their three sons, Glen, Wayne, and Ray, and Viola's mother, father, and brother were living with them in Petaluma. In July 1931 in Petaluma, Harley and Sis had another baby, a girl they named Ruth. On the 1940 census, Harley listed himself as a rancher. He died in 1966; Viola died in 1983. They are buried together at the Cypress Hill Memorial Park Cemetery in Petaluma.

Otto Orphus Winfrey: After Ethel's brother Otto was killed by the lightning strike, his wife Valeria and their two sons, Laverne and Merrell, lived with Valeria's parents, who were also homesteading near Kim. Laverne married DeEtta Green in 1945 in Andrix. He became a school teacher, eventually living in Greeley, Colorado, and teaching in Windsor, Colorado. Merrell made a lifetime career in the US Army and married a woman from Japan (name unknown). They had one son, Earl LeRoy. Merrell retired from the army and lived in Mira Loma,

California. Valeria died in 1953 and is buried in the Kim cemetery, along with Otto and their baby son Ralph.

Susan (Sue) Ellen Winfrey Priddy: Ethel's sister Sue and her husband, Bill Priddy, had six children. Sue and Bill went back and forth between Andrix and Wellington, Texas, where Bill's parents lived. Their first child, William Eugene Priddy, was born in 1917 in Two Buttes, Colorado. Their second, Helen Louise Priddy, was born in 1920 in Wellington. Zelma Mae Priddy was born in 1922 in Springfield, Colorado; Bennie Pauline Priddy in 1924 in Vernon, Texas; Billie Sue Priddy in 1928 in Vernon; and Donald Carlyle Priddy in 1930 in Amherst, Texas.

In 1936, Bill and Sue moved to Grove, Oklahoma. Their daughter Bennie Pauline had rheumatic heart disease, and they moved to Grove hoping that the climate there would be better for her. In Grove, Bill and Sue ran a boarding house for the men who were building the Grand River Dam. In 1938, they moved back to their farm in Amherst. Bennie Pauline succumbed to her rheumatic heart disease in 1940 and died at the age of sixteen.

In 1953, Sue and Bill divorced, and in 1954, Bill remarried. His second wife's name was Iva. Bill died in 1976; Iva is buried beside him. After the divorce, Sue moved to Springfield, Missouri, where she bought a large house that allowed her to rent rooms out as apartments. In the early 1960s, she married James Morgan, a man who had been renting one of her apartments. They lived happily together until Sue's death on April 12, 1969. She is buried in Springfield.

Emil Benjamin Winfrey: Ethel's brother Emil and his wife, Lola, left Colorado in 1929 and moved to Dalhart, Texas, where Emil acquired two trucks and began a truck hauling business. The trucking business struggled throughout the Great Depression, but Emil managed to find hauling opportunities by following the wheat harvests from Kansas to Nebraska and Montana, and the potato and bean harvest in Idaho. Ruby's husband, Verne Royse, joined Emil at the hauling business, and the two families traveled and camped together during those difficult times. Soon after Emil and his father-in-law, Wiley Winters, helped Ethel move to Flint, Oklahoma, Emil made the decision to move to warmer weather. In November 1935, he moved his family to Phoenix,

Arizona, where his trucking business flourished. For several years before and after World War II, the E.B. Winfrey Trucking Company was the largest trucking firm in the Phoenix valley. It was in Phoenix that Emil and Lola's two daughters, Margie and Ardith, married brothers. Margie married Dennis Hudson in 1941, and Ardith married Don Hudson in 1946. Dennis served in the US Air Force during WWII, and Don landed on Normandy Beach on D-Day with the Combat Engineers. They both returned home after the war.

In 1943, Emil and Lola had another daughter, whom they named Denah. Emil eventually sold his trucking business and bought two ensilage cutters, which he operated until the time of his death. He died on January 16, 1953, at age fifty-two. Denah was thirteen years old when her father died.

Ruby Estle Winfrey Royse: Ethel's sister Ruby and her husband, Verne M. Royse, had four sons and a daughter. After their first two sons, Don and Robert, were born, they left Berryville in an attempt to make a living during the Depression. Verne got into the trucking business, just as Emil had done. The 1940 census shows that Emil, his family, Ruby, and her family (including their mother, Blanch) were all living in Phoenix. Emil and Verne both listed their occupations as truck drivers. In 1939, Ruby and Verne had twin boys, Earl and Mearl, who were born in Phoenix. Ruby and Verne eventually moved their family to Gooding, Idaho, where their daughter, Sheryl, was born. Verne became the sheriff of Gooding County.

On August 8, 1968, Verne was thrown from his horse while riding in a county fair parade. He struck his head on the pavement of Main Street, a fatal injury. Ruby died in 2004 at the age of ninety-four. She is buried in Elmwood Cemetery in Gooding.

THE REST OF THE REST OF THE STORY

Leander (Lee) Roseling Bailey: Leander (Lee) and Bessie lived the rest of their lives together in San Bernardino, California. After moving to San Bernardino, they had another child, a girl named Betty. Jeanie Wilson conducted a long search for documentation in all surrounding states, but there is no evidence that Lee and Bessie ever married. However, Ethel did finally file for divorce from Lee in 1947, so that she could remarry. Lee died in San Bernardino in 1967. The state of California did not, and does not, recognize common-law marriage; therefore, it appears that Lee and Bessie were never legally married. Lee was buried at Mt. View Cemetery in San Bernardino. His headstone says "Leo Bailey." Bessie died eleven years after Lee. She is buried next to him. Lee and Bessie's son, William C. Bailey, died in 1993 at the age of seventy-two and was also buried in Mt. View Cemetery. Their daughter, Betty Carol Bailey Strout, died in 2006 at the age of seventy-six. She was buried in Riverside, California. William C. was almost ten years older than Betty.

The 1939 San Bernardino City Directory shows that Lee and Bessie were living on East Eleventh Street. Lee listed himself this time as Leo R. Bailey, auto wrecker. The census for the following year showed Leo Bailey at age forty-three, born in Missouri, married (this is true—he was still married to Ethel), an automobile-parts salesman and homeowner, living with Bess Bailey, age forty-three, born in Kansas. Living with them was William Bailey, age eighteen, born in Kansas, listed as a parking-lot attendant, and Betty Bailey, age nine, born in California.

Lee completed a WWII Draft Registration, listing his name as Leander Roseling Bailey, date of birth March 1895, born Mt. Grove, Missouri. He listed his address as 2595 Valencia, San Bernardino, California, and his occupation as rancher—chicken business. The 1949 San Bernardino City Directory shows Leo Bailey, salesman, and Bessie B. Bailey, still living at 2595 Valencia.

Frank Parise: Frank Parise, Bessie's ex-husband, remarried soon after he was granted a divorce from Bessie. His second wife's name was Bridget Delaney. He became a federal prohibition agent in Nevada and gained quite a notorious reputation. One newspaper article referred to him as "Frank Parise, giant sledgehammer wielder of the Nevada prohibition squad." He later opened a private-detective agency in Sacramento, California. It appears that he never had any children of his own, and it is unknown what happened to his adopted daughter, Lois, who was listed as living with him and Bessie in Trinidad on the 1920 census. The census shows that Lois was six years old in 1920; she was never listed on another census. Frank and Bridget were in California on the 1930 census. No children were listed. After Bridget died in 1937, Frank moved to Galveston, Texas, where he died in 1965.

Frank H. Hall (the man who got the title to Lee and Ethel's land in 1928): Frank H. Hall was a lawyer in Trinidad, Colorado. Records show that he represented a company involved in a dispute over the drilling of helium gas in commercial quantities on southeastern Colorado plains land. In all likelihood, Frank Hall saw the opportunity to take title of multiple parcels of land in 1927, because of unpaid taxes. It is possible that he was speculating that the land would become valuable because of natural gas and helium reservoirs. It appears that he never visited the land he had gained title to, where Ethel and her children were living, and he may never have known they were living there; if he did know, he apparently did not care. There are no records that the land was ever used for anything other than grazing cattle. Today, the land homesteaded by Lee and Ethel belongs to the federal government.

The town of Kim, Colorado: When the Dust Bowl hit the southeastern plains of Colorado, the population of Kim began to dwindle. The dust and the Depression stopped all growth of that small town; however, Kim has survived. Today, Highway 160 still runs through Kim, right beside the Kim cemetery where many Winfreys are buried. Today's Kim, population sixty-six in 2016, has a post office, a general store, and a complete school system for grades kindergarten through twelve. The high school gymnasium was finally completed under the WPA, along with two other school buildings. The gymnasium was, for years, the gathering place for all events for the people living in Kim. Kim is located within the Comanche National Grasslands.

The community of Andrix, Colorado: Andrix can still be found on maps, yet there are only three buildings still standing there, all of which were abandoned long ago. The Andrix store built by Harley Winfrey is gone, as is the Andrix school. However, the rock building near the school, which housed the teacher on one side and served as a shelter for students' horses on the other, is still standing. The Quaker church is gone, but the foundation can still be seen. The green building in the photograph on page 94 was probably some type of automobile garage/repair shop. There is a weathered wooden structure behind the garage, probably a house, barely standing. The Andrix cemetery, located on a hill about a half mile from where the store was, still remains. The population of Andrix is said to never have risen above thirty.

In 1937, two years after Ethel and her children left Andrix, Fred and Icie Cox sold the Andrix store to Jess and Nora Allen, who ran it together until Jess's death in 1950. Nora then ran the store alone. In 1955, the store was ransacked and robbed by two intruders, who were arrested near Kim shortly after the robbery. One of the robbers was a former Andrix resident whom Mrs. Allen had known since his birth. By 1960, Nora was the only inhabitant of Andrix. She died in 1973.

Someone has painted the words "Andrix, gone but not forgotten" on the front of the garage / repair shop that is still standing in Andrix. Andrix is listed on many Colorado historical websites as a ghost town.

The dugout, rock house, and wooden house on Ethel's claim have all been filled in, torn down, and hauled off. Today there is no sign that anyone ever homesteaded that claim.

The Prairie Star School: The Prairie Star School building is gone, but the building that was the teacher's quarters and horse shelter, which Robert helped build in 1933, is still standing along Highway 160, about five miles from Kim.

The land in Colorado: During Franklin Roosevelt's presidency, the homesteading movement initiated by Abraham Lincoln came to a halt. With the Taylor Grazing Act of 1934, the government withheld remaining public lands from homesteaders. The act also authorized the Department of the Interior to establish grazing districts and manage a grazing-permit system. Under the Land Utilization Program (LUP), the government eventually purchased more than 4.7 million acres of submarginal farmland and overgrazed rangeland in the West. Local grazing associations managed the purchased lands jointly, together with other publicly and privately owned lands, altogether improving more than thirty million acres. In 1953, the management of lands purchased by the LUP was transferred from the US Soil Conservation Service to the US Forest Service. On June 20, 1960, the lands in southeastern Colorado became part of the Comanche National Grasslands.

When Ethel and her children left their homestead in Colorado in 1935, the area still did not have electricity. Electricity was not available in the Andrix area until ten years later when, because of the Rural Electrification Act, it finally arrived.

All of Claude's land was divided and passed on to his children, Irene, Creeda, Benjamin, and Raymond. Most of it was eventually passed on to his grandchildren, who still, to this day, own it. It is all now part of the Comanche National Grasslands and is leased for cattle grazing.

The Towner Bus Tragedy: The Towner Bus Tragedy of 1931 was the worst tragedy in the Colorado school system until the 1999 shootings at Columbine High School in Littleton, Colorado. In 1961, a monument was put up to mark the place where the Towner bus had stalled. The bus driver and the five children who froze to death in the blizzard are buried together in the Holly cemetery in Holly, Colorado, where a large monument and individual headstones mark their graves. In an interesting turn of events, one of the men who joined in the search for the school bus in the middle of that Colorado blizzard, and who helped rescue the surviving children and get them to a place of safety, eventually moved to Siloam Springs, Arkansas, where he built homes in what was called the "Coons Addition." His name was E. N. Coons. He was eighteen years old when he and his father joined in the search for the lost school bus. Later in his life, he wrote his story about the tragedy; his book is entitled *36 Hours of Hell.*

ACKNOWLEDGMENTS

Jeanie Wilson – As I said in the beginning, without my dear friend Jeanie Wilson, I could not have written this book. She amazed me day after day with the information and documents she was somehow able to find. Imagine my surprise when she found things like Inez Bailey's death certificate, the Bureau of Land Management serial patents for the homesteaded land in Colorado, and Frank and Bessie Parise's divorce papers—to name just a few. When I first started giving Jeanie names and dates, the only thing I knew about Bessie Parise was her first name. Jeanie somehow found that Bessie was married to Frank Parise, and that her maiden name was James. The details about Bessie are only in my story because of Jeanie.

Donna Jones Pearce (Claude Winfrey's granddaughter, and Irene Winfrey Jones's daughter) – When I found Donna, she graciously sent me the *only* copy she had of her mother's book. It was like striking gold to me. Irene's book answered so many questions I had about my grandmother's life on the Great Plains. That only copy of Irene's book is now safely back with Donna in Arizona, and I have a newfound cousin whom I love.

Ardith Winfrey Hudson (Emil's daughter) – Because of Donna Pearce, I found out about Ardith, another cousin in Arizona. Ardith has been another gold mine of information. She had pictures that I never could have dreamed existed, and with the help of her granddaughter, Donna Wild, she graciously shared them with me. Ardith is another newly found cousin I love.

Barbara Mangrum (Margie Bailey's daughter) – Barbara spent time answering lots of questions and constantly encouraging me to keep going. She wanted this story told as badly as I did. Thanks, Barbara!

Doug Bailey and his wife Joyce (Robert's son and daughter-in-law) – Doug's recollection of things he learned from his dad helped me, many times, add to the story and put the pieces together. And his sweet wife, Joyce, helped with her emails of constant encouragement.

Other cousins – Many of my cousins spent time on the phone and sending emails, providing me with information about their parents. Thanks go to Donna Bailey Kowalski, Mary Sharon Lynch Woods, Mearl Royse, Lynn Noble Mills, and Joan Noble Michael.

Bub Autry of Kim, Colorado – Mr. Autry is a lifetime resident of the LaJunta / Kim, Colorado, area and is a walking "book of knowledge" about that part of Colorado. He picked up his phone without fail and was always kind enough to patiently answer all my questions.

Fran Jackson Henry Endicott (my sister) – Fran went with me to Kim and Andrix, Colorado. Thanks to Fran, I got to see where this story took place.

Brandon Gabel (my son) – Brandon helped me find Donna Pearce. Thanks, Brandon!

Made in the USA
San Bernardino, CA
09 February 2019